Murt Stones.

The Window and Bed Sketchbook

The Window and Bed Sketchbook

Wendy Baker

SHOESTRING BOOK COMPANY

P.O.Box 7610, Hungerford, RG17 0WE, United Kingdom
Telephone/Fax: +44(0) 1488 681599
Email: info@shoestringbooks.co.uk
www.shoestringbooks.co.uk

Other books by Wendy Baker

The Curtain Sketchbook
The Bed Sketchbook
The Curtain Sketchbook 2
The Curtain and Fabric Selector

Illustrations by Chrissie Carriere
With grateful thanks for her inspired illustrations and her bounding enthusiasm!

For interior design commissions Wendy Baker can be contacted by Email...
wendybaker@shoestringbooks.co.uk

ISBN 0-9532939-4-7

Published by Shoestring Book Company U.K.

Printed and bound by Bath Press, Bath U.K.

CONTENTS

INTRODUCTION

THE WINDOW AND BED SKETCHBOOK is the 4th book in the series and I am sure, as with the other books, you will find it invaluable when choosing a style for your curtains, beds or other soft furnishings. It will, I hope, open up new areas that you may not have thought of before.

There are so many points to take into consideration when choosing a style for curtains for instance, the shape of the windows, height of the ceiling, does the room face North? If you have a blind inside the recess will it block out too much light? The whole thing can be quite bewildering.

Rushing off to your local bookshop and thumbing through decorating books and magazines doesn't really help, if anything it tends to lead to more confusion. So relax, go through THE WINDOW AND BED SKETCHBOOK, look for inspiration, it's all there.

Maybe you really don't want curtains in your home or office, then choose blinds or have a colourful screen at the windows instead. The book is full of alternative ideas. The sketches are, as usual, black line drawings so that the designs are completely clear, you can colour them if you wish, but I suggest you look at your windows first, choose between curtains or blinds, pick the style - then decide on a colour to fit in with your existing colour scheme or a new colour if starting from scratch. Finally collect all this together and head for your nearest fabric store or showroom. Hopefully everything will fall into place and you will have reached your goal with virtually no problems and very few tears.

There is a very important part of this book dedicated to TRIMMINGS (passementerie). Trimmings can be very expensive, the sky is the limit, but there is also a vast range of inexpensive ones in the shops. Don't be nervous about using them, they can often help to 'pull a room together' achieving the last finishing touch. If you have put fringing for instance on your curtains, perhaps echo the same theme onto the cushions or the sofa - but don't overdo it.

When I am designing a room, and perhaps my budget is not very large, I might cheat a little and buy an inexpensive fabric, choose a simple shaped curtain but emphasise the simple lines with a wonderful flamboyant braid - it always works - be brave - experiment.

When you come to the section on BEDS you will see that there are plenty of ideas to redesign your bed by buying a new headboard or some new bed linen, but there are some useful ideas if you are thinking of buying a new bed. The children's section illustrates how essential it is to have lots of storage space around the bed as well as it being fun. The adults beds can be cosy or sophisticated, as you wish, but most of all the bed must be right for you. If you want a hard bed, make sure you lie on it before buying it, it may be too hard for you which will lead to back problems.

For ultimate luxury why not buy a feather mattress to go on top of your own mattress .... there's an address at the back of the book, check it out, that's real luxury for you!

Throughout the book you will find on the left hand page BASIC DESIGNS with VARIATIONS on the right hand side. When choosing curtains for instance, look as the BASIC WINDOW SHAPE, identifying your window as close as possible, then choose your HEADING and POLE or TRACKING - which ever you prefer. When you have made your selection you simply turn to VARIATIONS opposite you chosen heading - it's very easy. It works in a similar way for TRIMMINGS and BEDS.

The final decisions I have to leave to you, after all you have to live with.it - I don't!
All I have tried to do is to make your choice a little easier with some new ideas and suggestions.

Basic window

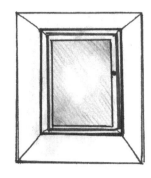

Recessed window

Double cottage window

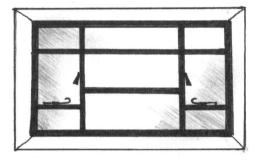

1930's metal frame

Georgian sash

Arched Georgian sash

Half glazed door

Sliding patio doors

French doors with side windows

French doors in bay

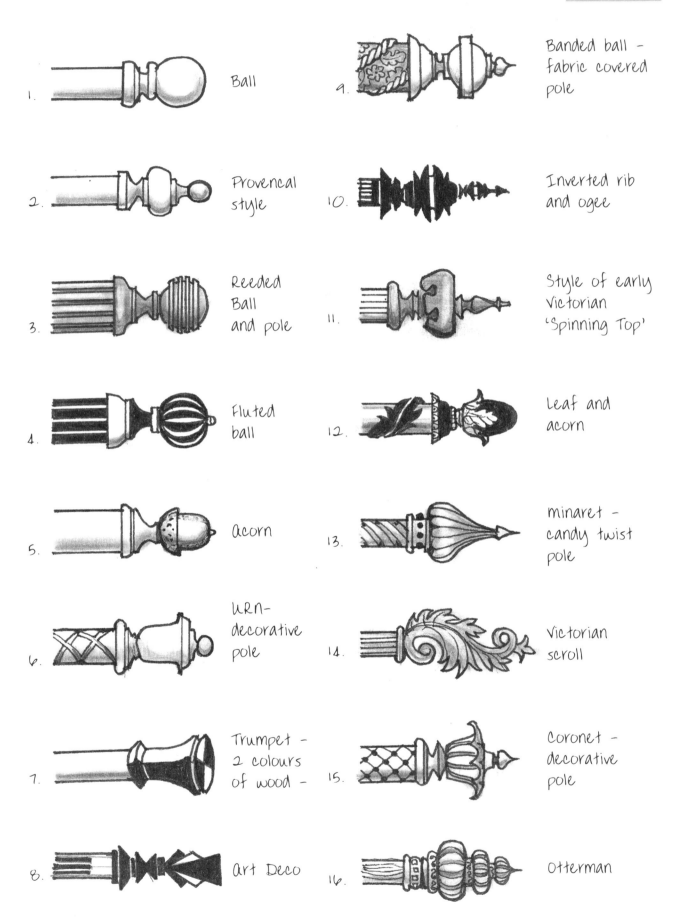

1. Ball

2. Provencal style

3. Reeded Ball and pole

4. Fluted ball

5. Acorn

6. URN - decorative pole

7. Trumpet - 2 colours of wood -

8. Art Deco

9. Banded ball - fabric covered pole

10. Inverted rib and ogee

11. Style of early Victorian 'Spinning Top'

12. Leaf and acorn

13. minaret - candy twist pole

14. Victorian scroll

15. Coronet - decorative pole

16. Otterman

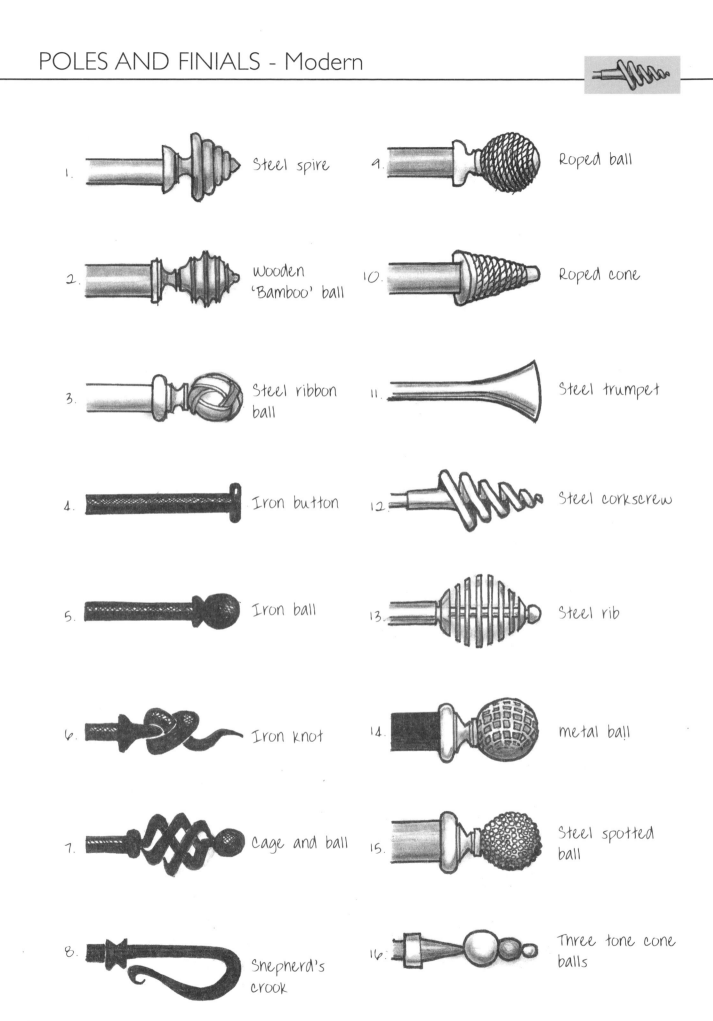

1. Steel spire

2. Wooden 'Bamboo' ball

3. Steel ribbon ball

4. Iron button

5. Iron ball

6. Iron knot

7. Cage and ball

8. Shepherd's crook

9. Roped ball

10. Roped cone

11. Steel trumpet

12. Steel corkscrew

13. Steel rib

14. metal ball

15. Steel spotted ball

16. Three tone cone balls

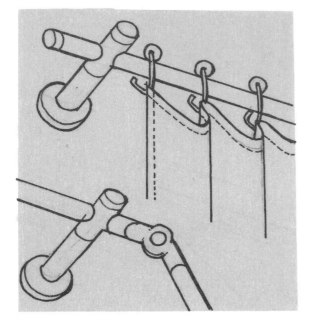

1. Stainless steel roller-line pole – can also be used for angles

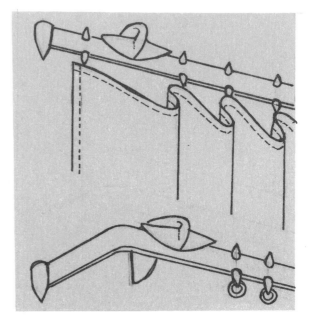

2. Stainless steel flat pole – curves for a bay window

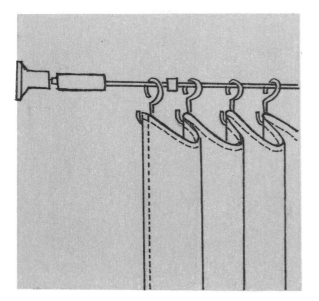

3. Tension wire system used from wall to wall

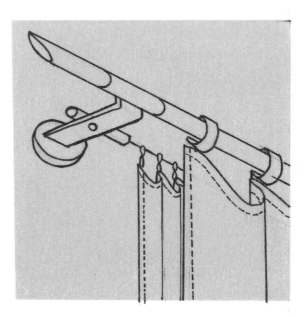

4. Stainless steel pole – can be used with tension wire for second curtain

BASIC CURTAIN HEADINGS

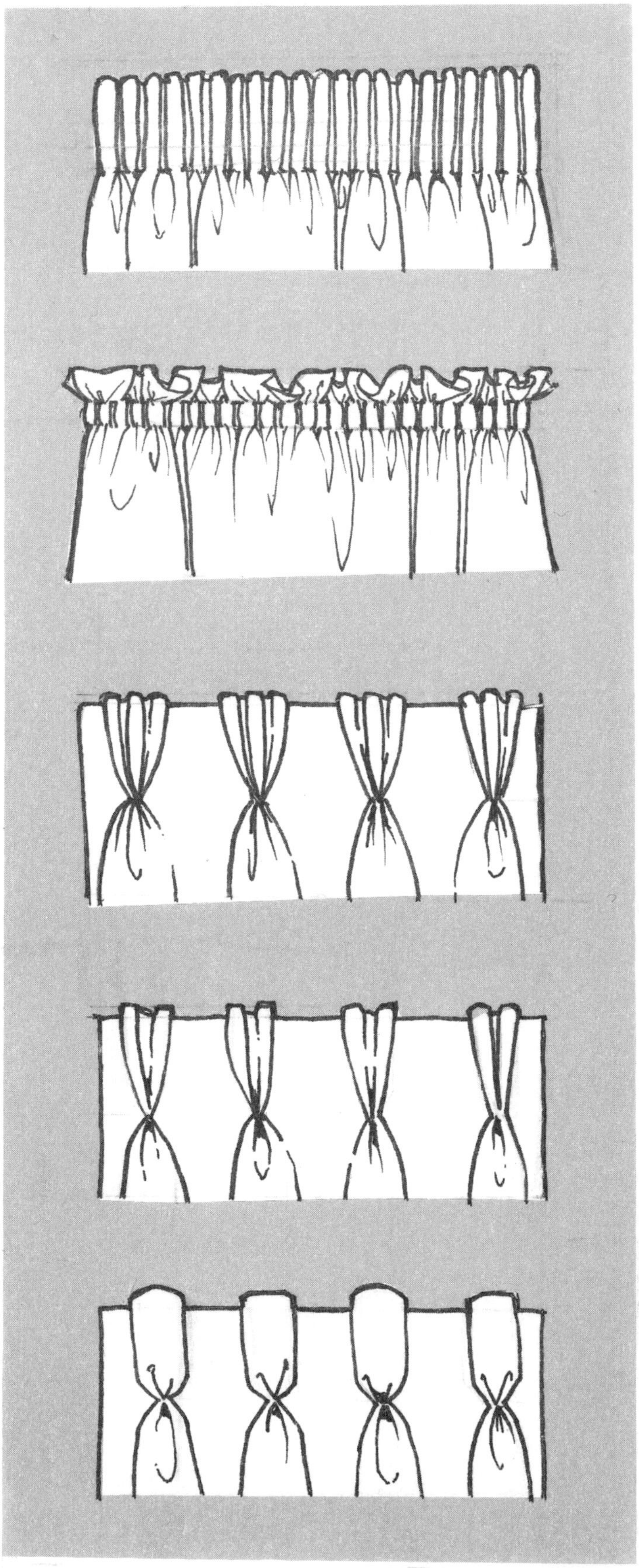

1. Pencil pleat

2. unstructured

3. Triple pinch pleat

4. Double pinch pleat

5. Goblet or Tulip

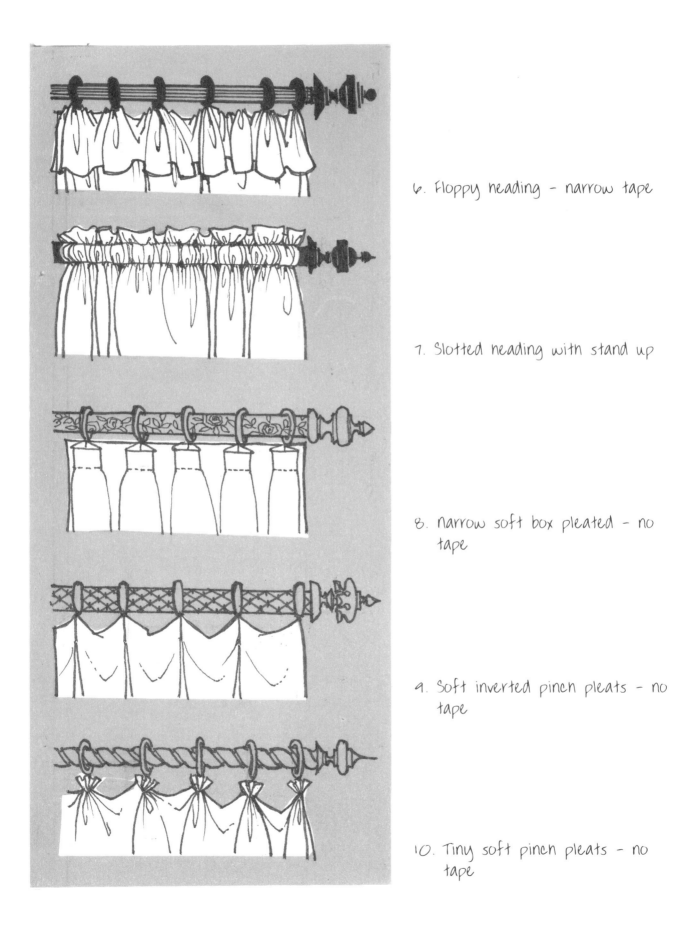

6. Floppy heading – narrow tape

7. Slotted heading with stand up

8. narrow soft box pleated – no tape

9. Soft inverted pinch pleats – no tape

10. Tiny soft pinch pleats – no tape

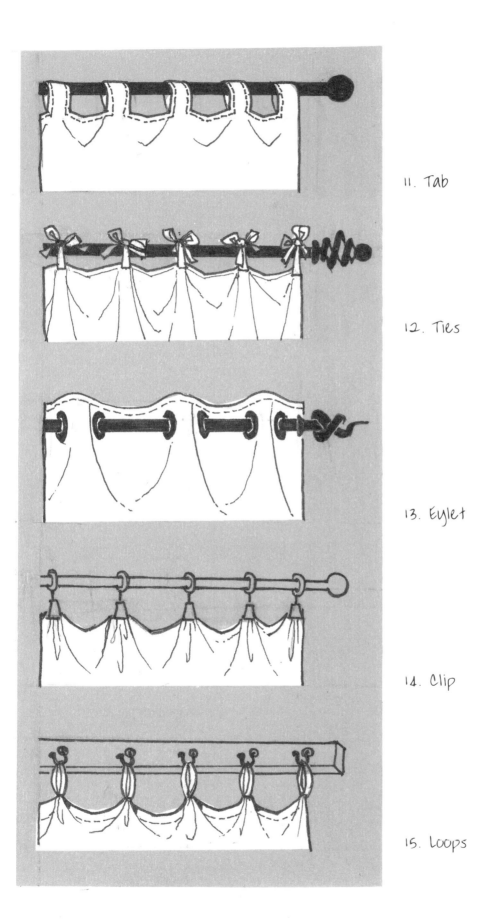

11. Tab

12. Ties

13. Eylet

14. Clip

15. Loops

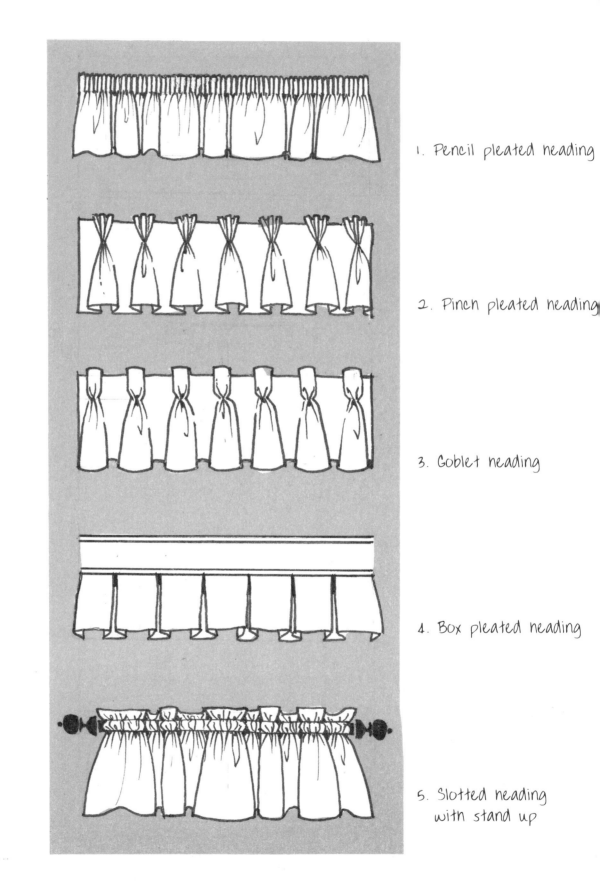

1. Pencil pleated heading

2. Pinch pleated heading

3. Goblet heading

4. Box pleated heading

5. Slotted heading with stand up

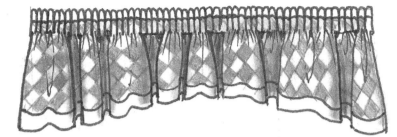

1. Drooping sides – contrast band on hem

2. Drooping sides – contrast bands on top and hem with buttons

3. Bullion fringing and knotted ropes

4. Emphasize the shape with knotted ropes

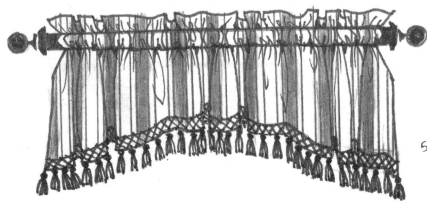

5. Soft and gathered with trellis fringing on the hem

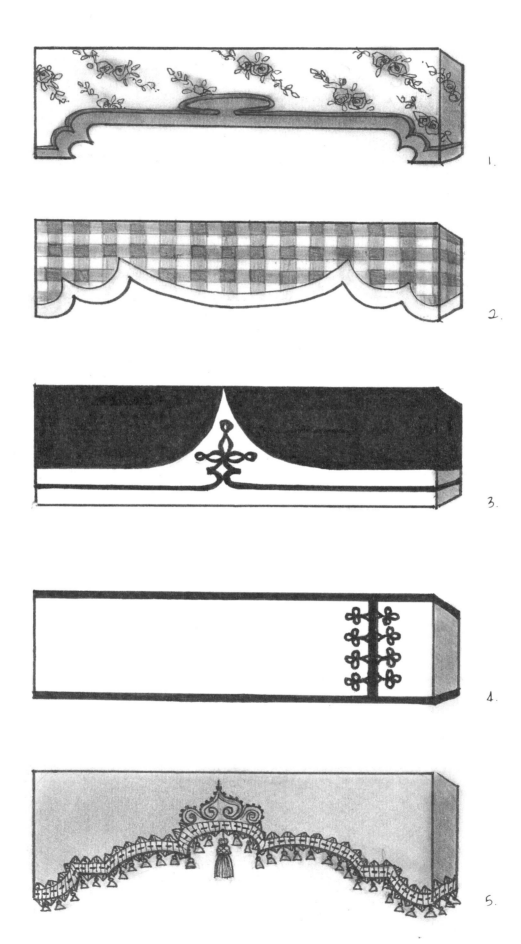

1.

2.

3.

4.

5.

1.

2.

3.

4.

5.

6.

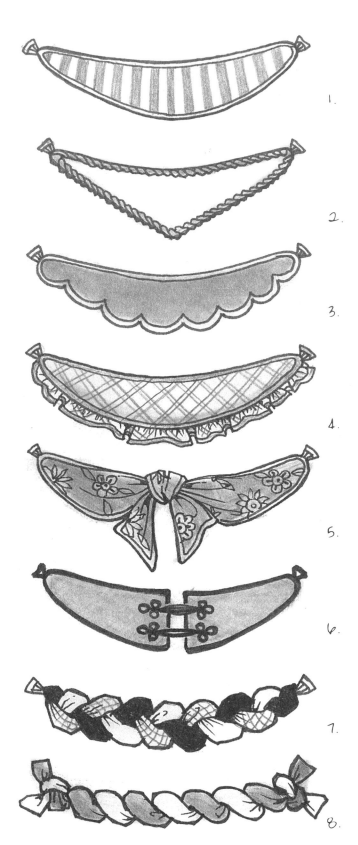

1.

2.

3.

4.

5.

6.

7.

8.

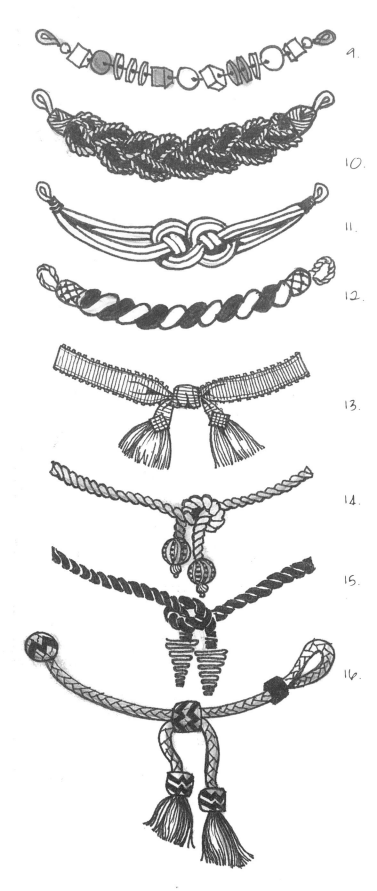

9.

10.

11.

12.

13.

14.

15.

16.

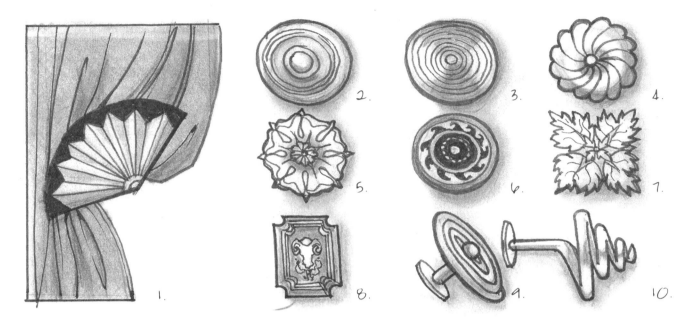

HOLD-BACKS can be found in a variety of materials - wood - metal - leather - resin. They neatly hold back the curtain allowing more light into the room

OMBRES or EMBRACES gather the curtain in a hook shaped 'Embrace' dressing the curtain and letting in more light

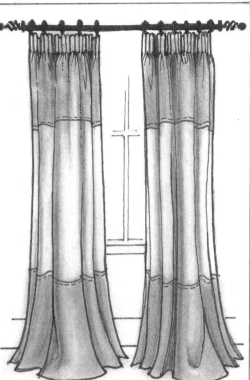

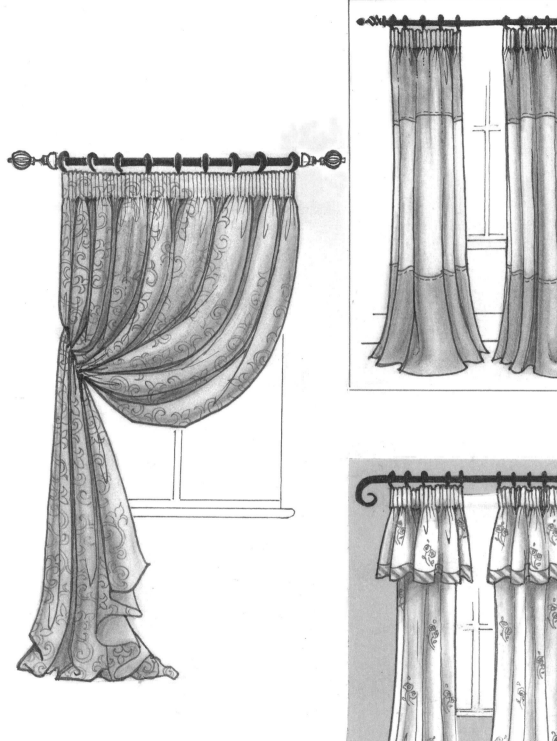

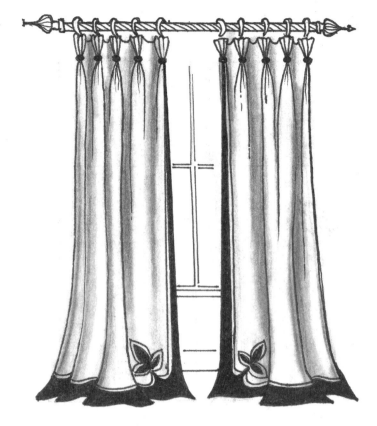

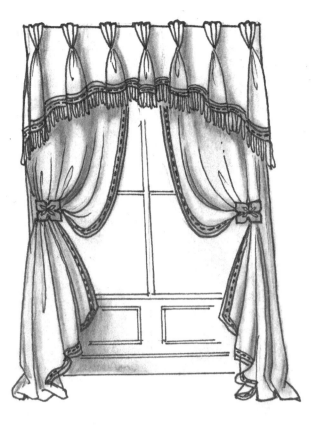

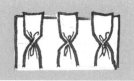

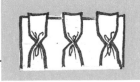

Contrast square buttons to accentuate the heading

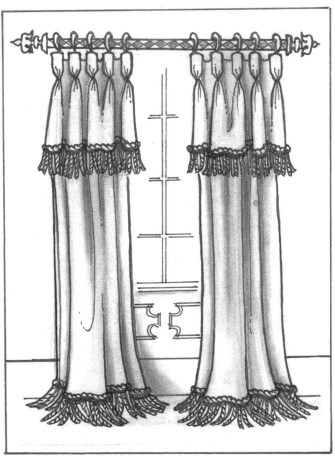

Heavy bullion fringe to emphasize the simple lines

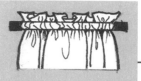

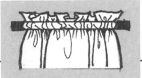

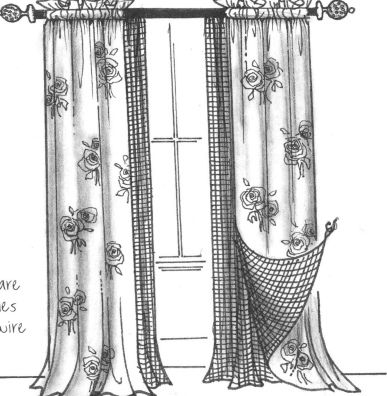

The flowered curtains are
dressed – the check ones
behind are on tension wire
and close

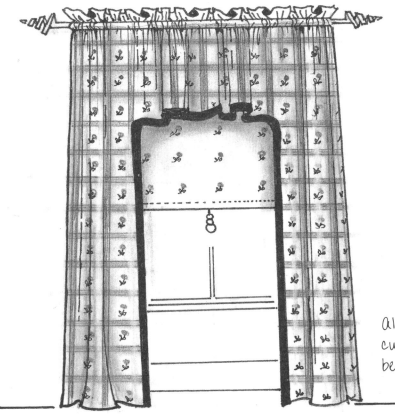

All in one valance and
curtains with blind
behind which closes

29

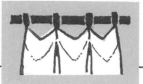

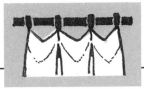

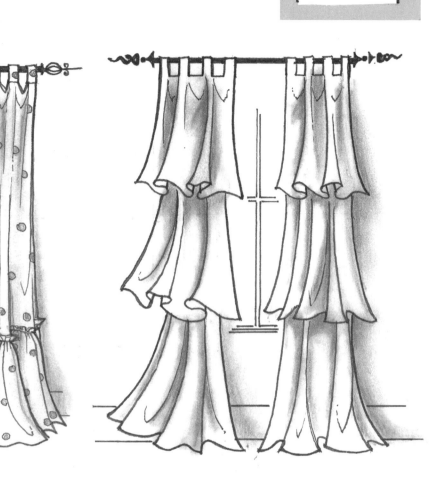

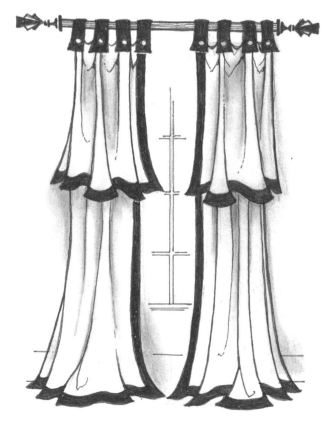

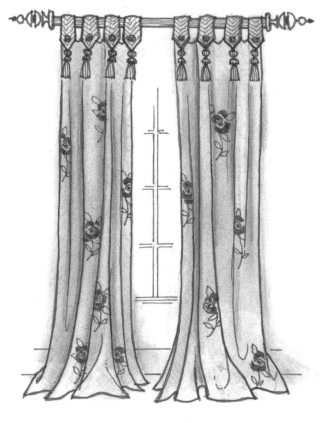

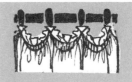

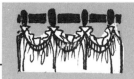

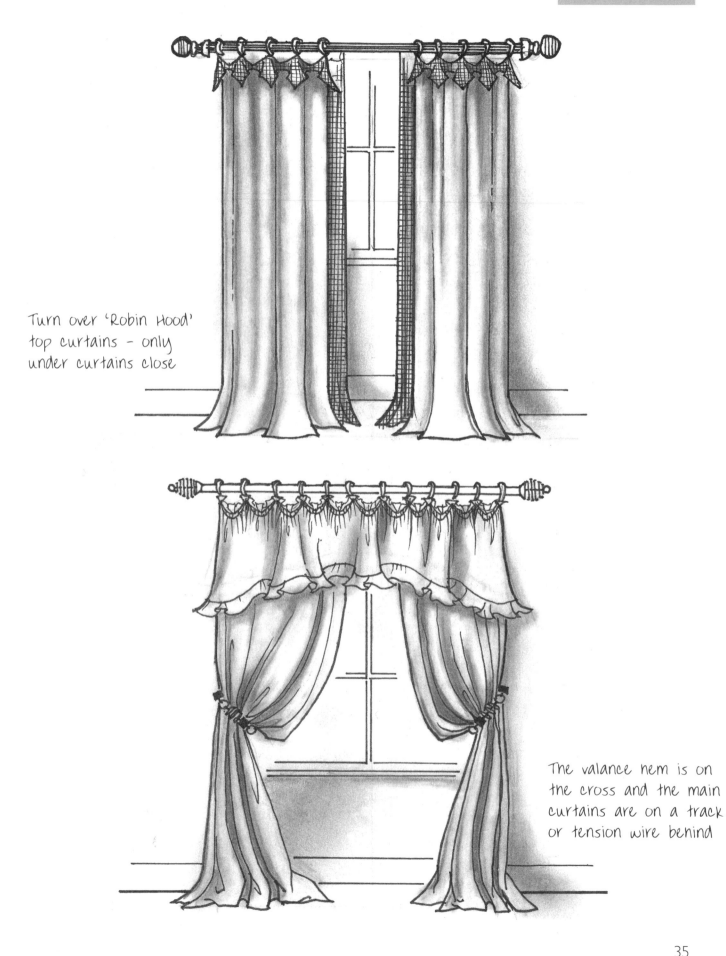

Turn over 'Robin Hood' top curtains – only under curtains close

The valance hem is on the cross and the main curtains are on a track or tension wire behind

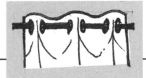

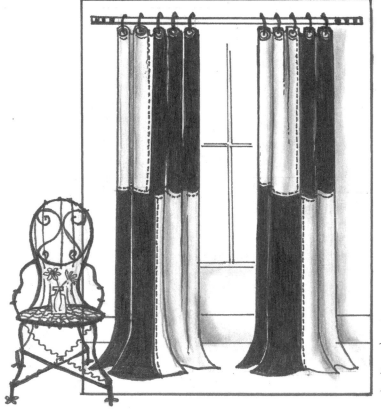

Two toned curtains with saddle-stitched seams - fabulous in suede and unlined

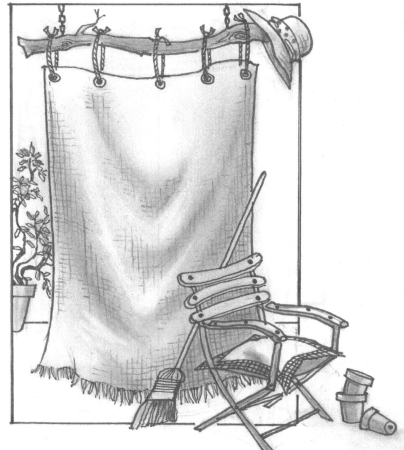

Hang an old piece of sacking up with ropes on a branch - just for fun...

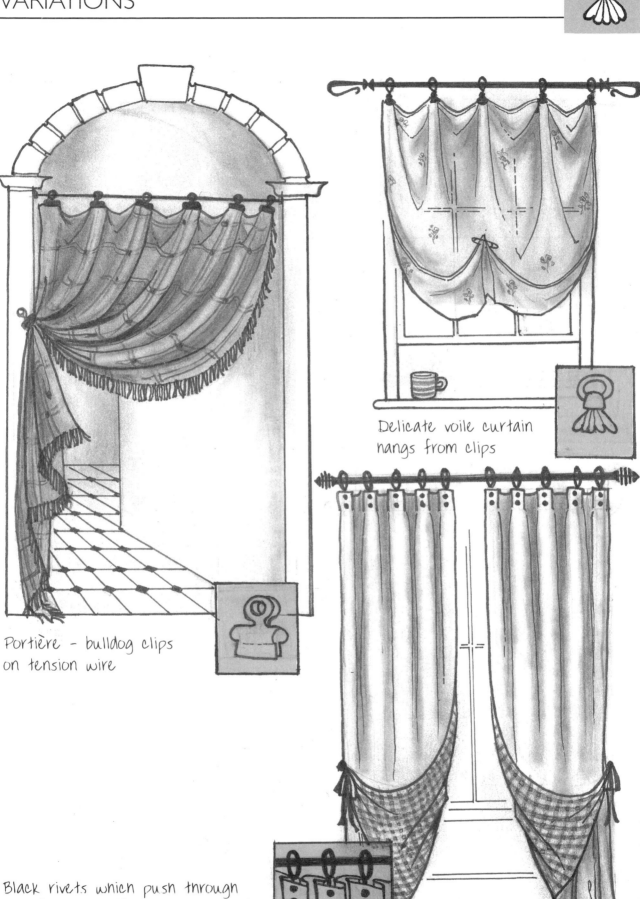

Delicate voile curtain
hangs from clips

Portière - bulldog clips
on tension wire

Black rivets which push through
any fabric can form several
different kinds of headings

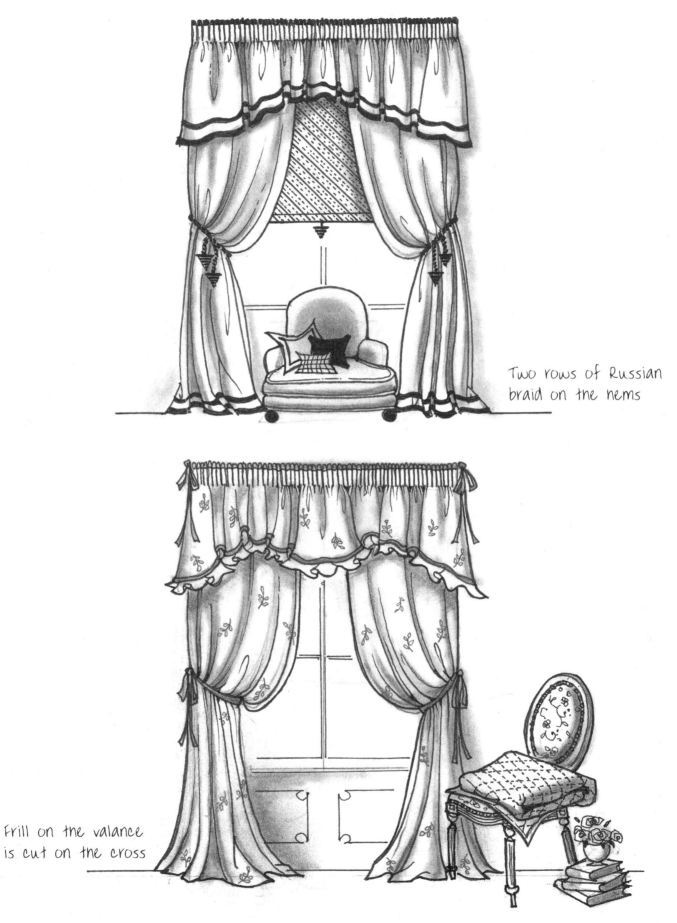

Two rows of Russian
braid on the hems

Frill on the valance
is cut on the cross

Valance with deep tucks - feathers fall from
plaited suede - saddle-stiched edges

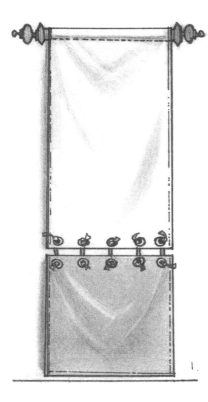

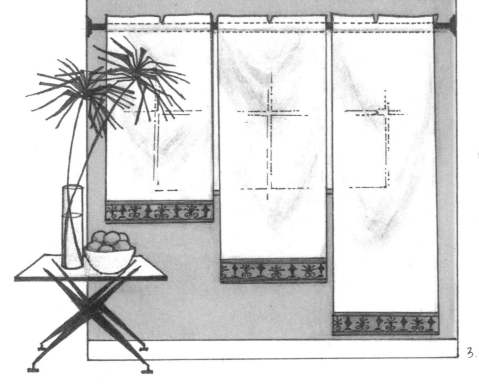

1. Eyelet holes – leather thonging
2. Window or wall hanging
3. Opaque panels to defuse the light
4. Room divider

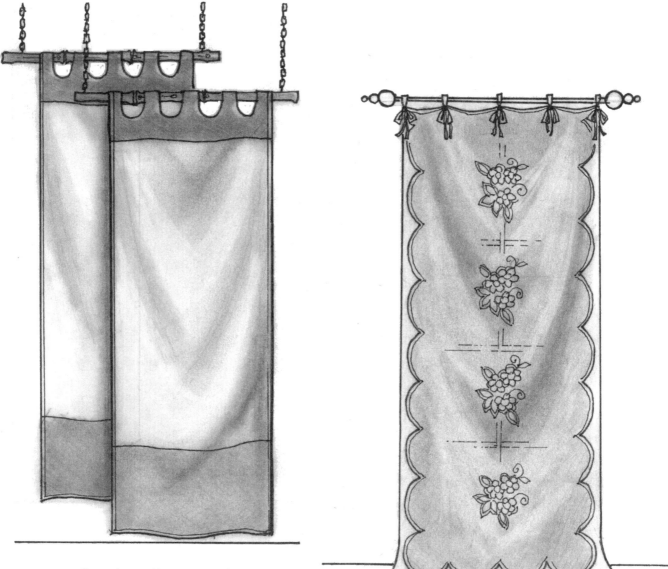

Two tone linen panels

Appliquéd organza panel

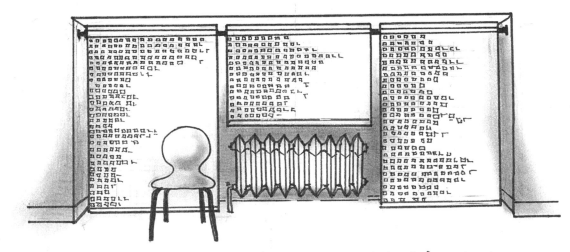

1. Three translucent window panels used to defuse light or hide an unwanted view

2. Panels can be fixed into frames to act as cupboard doors

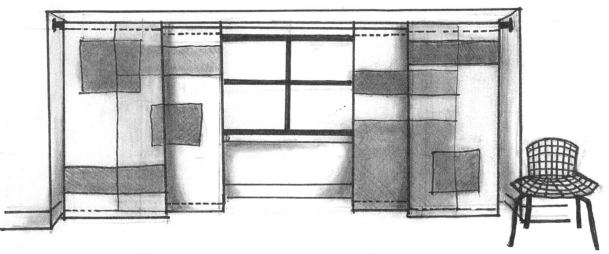

3. Colourful geometric panels are slotted on to a sliding panel system

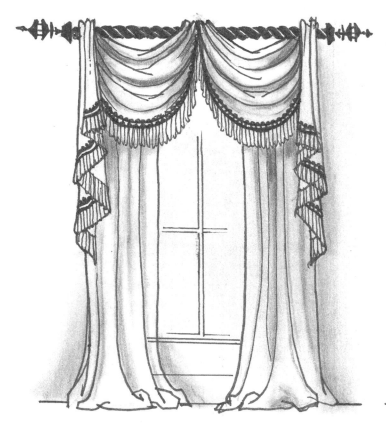

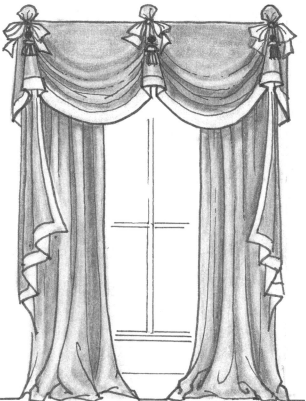

Swags and tails in the right room say it all – but don't overdo them!

Black and white checkerboard fabric on the covered
lath and curtain edges

Curtains on contemporary angled steel poles

Deep valance with droopy sides – contrast edge
and matching buttons

Softly gathered valance – knotted rope top –
bullion fringed hems

a covered lath is a narrow strip of wood - covered in fabric
- and attached to a pelmet board to conceal the curtain rails

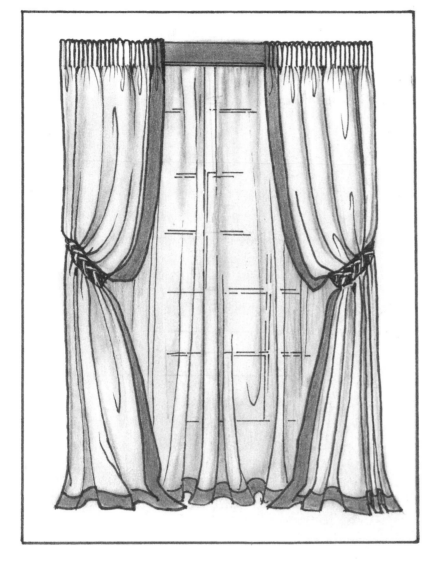

Use a contrast fabric or ribbons on the lath and the leading edges as well as the hems of both curtains

A covered lath works well when there are beams above the window

Heavy object

Window seat

Radiator

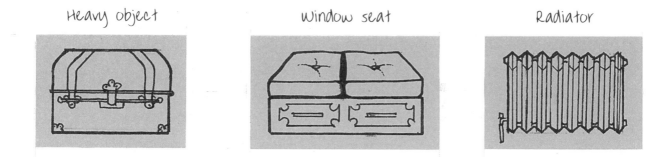

Above are three reasons why curtains could not be drawn across a window – in these cases use dressed curtains and blinds or simply leave clear

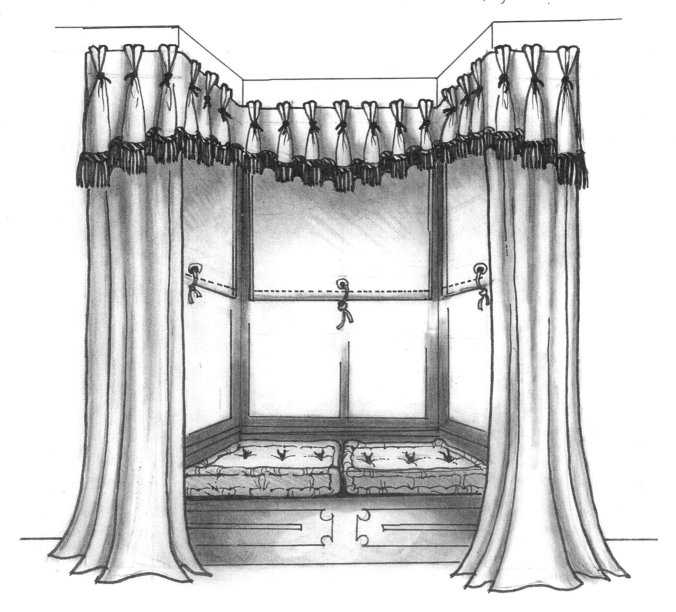

Roll-up blind with check lining and ties to match the band on the valance

One sided curtain with holland roller blind – scalloped edge bound with rope

...hide it behind a pair of
translucent slotted curtains
on brass rods

a small window sometimes
serves no purpose so...

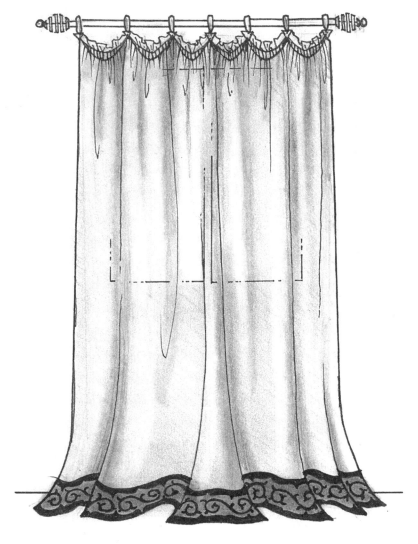

...hide it behind a long voile
curtain - also adds height to the room

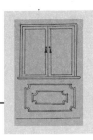

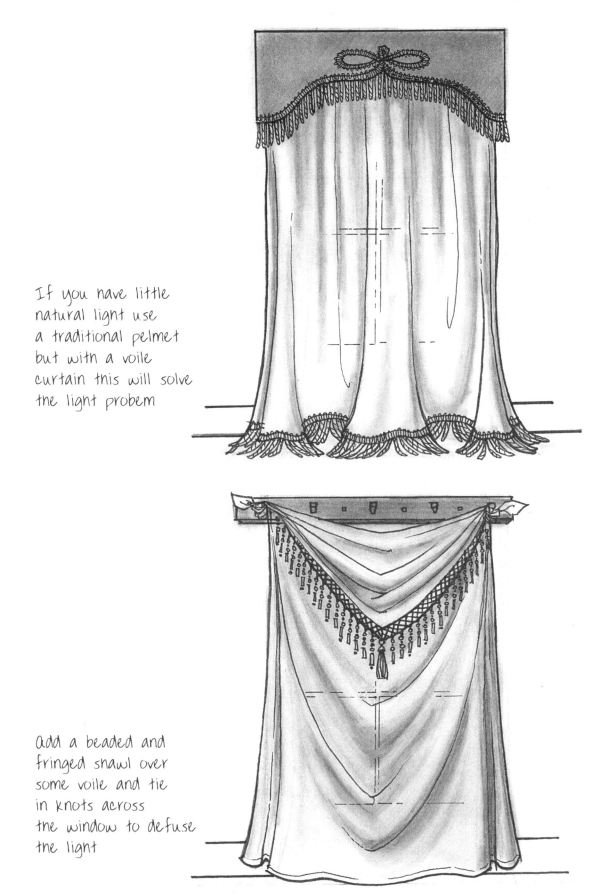

If you have little
natural light use
a traditional pelmet
but with a voile
curtain this will solve
the light probem

Add a beaded and
fringed shawl over
some voile and tie
in knots across
the window to defuse
the light

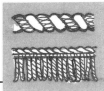

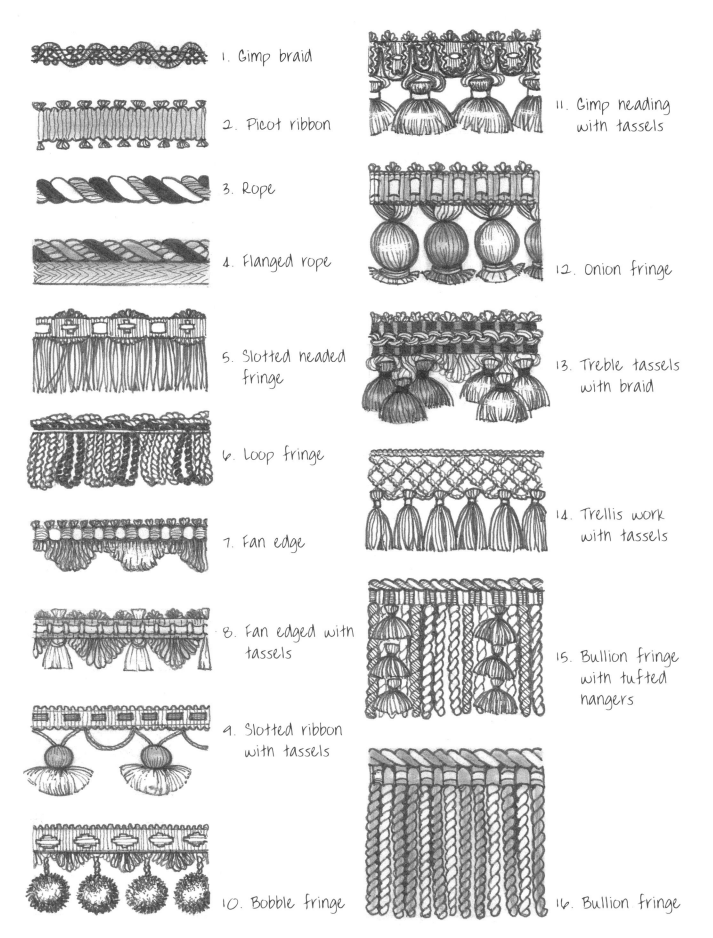

1. Gimp braid

2. Picot ribbon

3. Rope

4. Flanged rope

5. Slotted headed fringe

6. Loop fringe

7. Fan edge

8. Fan edged with tassels

9. Slotted ribbon with tassels

10. Bobble fringe

11. Gimp heading with tassels

12. Onion fringe

13. Treble tassels with braid

14. Trellis work with tassels

15. Bullion fringe with tufted hangers

16. Bullion fringe

59

1. Jacquard braid

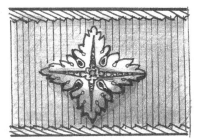

2. Ribbed braid with metal motif

3. Greek key braid

4. Scrolled jacquard ribbon

5. Woven leather

6. Crystal beads or satin ribbon

7. Bead fringe

8. Looped beads on gimp

9. Long strings of beads

10. Assorted crystal beads on satin ribbon

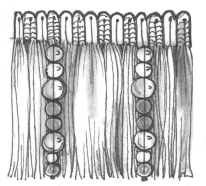

11. Cut fringe with beaded hangers

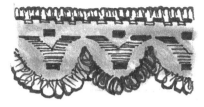

1. Van Dyke edging

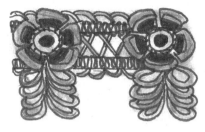

2. Jasmin fringe

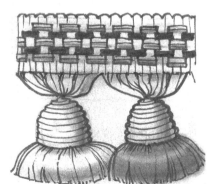

3. Decorative lace edging

4. Tassel fringe

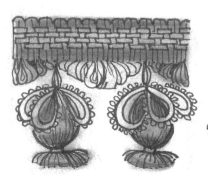

5. Jasmin tassel fringe

6. Gimp headed acorn fringe

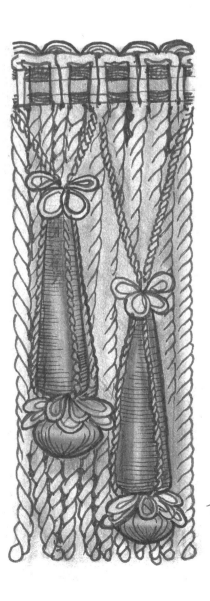

7. Bullion fringe with neoClassical hangers

The Classics

1. Acorn pull-cord
2. Rosette with acorn
3. Exotic tassels

Beaded tassels

Key tassels

Slim contemporary tassels

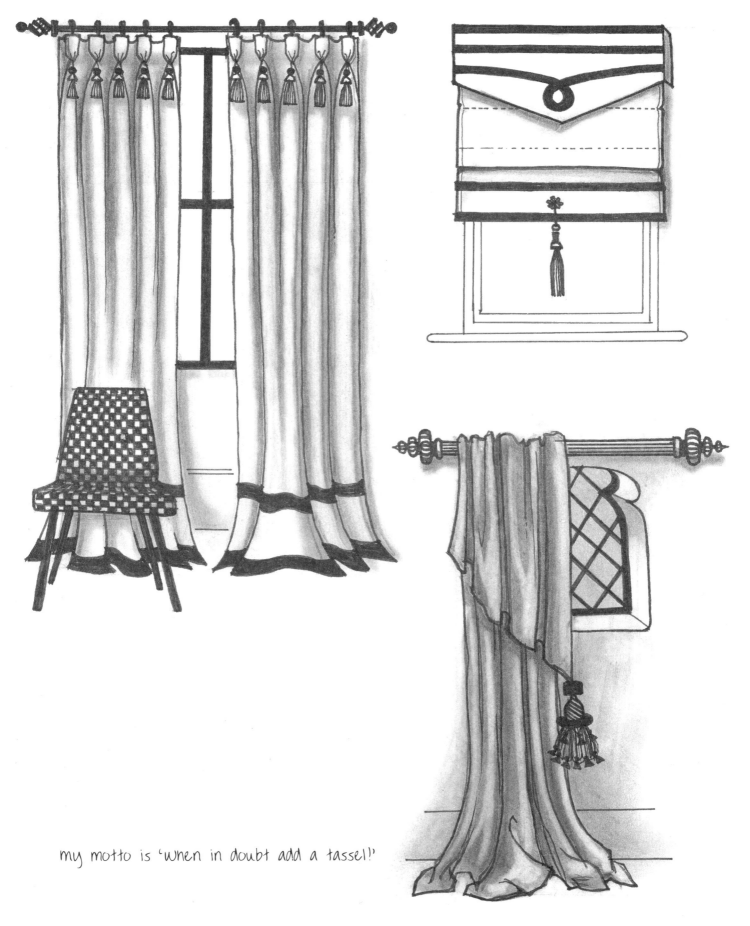

my motto is 'when in doubt add a tassel!'

BULLION FRINGE

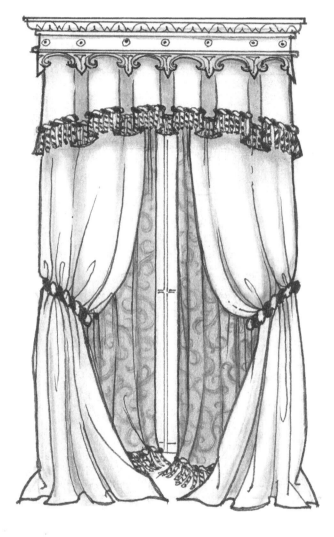

1. Carved wooden pelmet with box pleats — finishing with a heavy bullion fringing

2. Flamboyant patterned velvet curtains and pelmet — edged in bullion fringe with neoClassical hangers

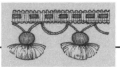

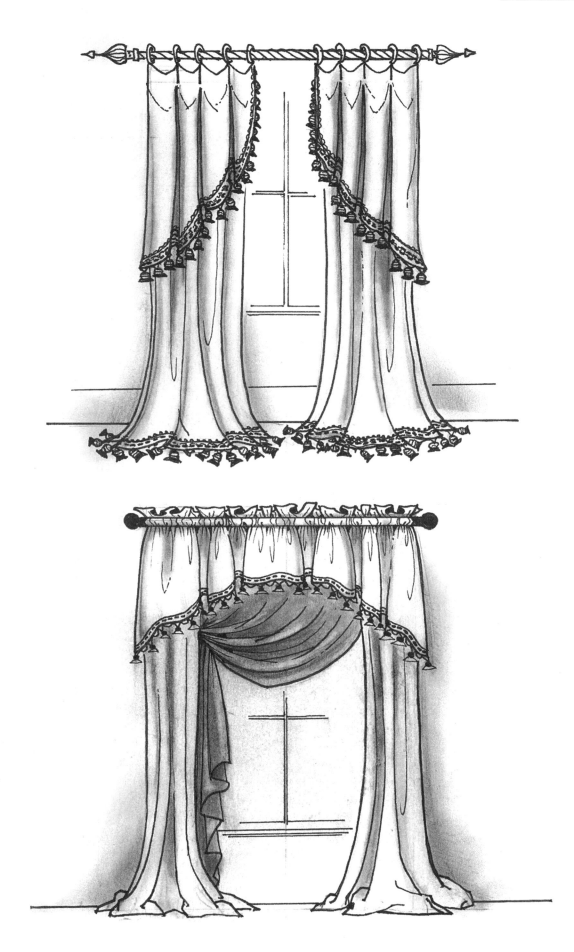

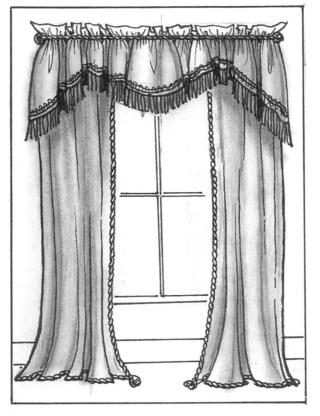

Knotted rope with long fringing – add rope to edges and hem

Quilted valance edged with rope – also on leading edge to emphasize the simple shap

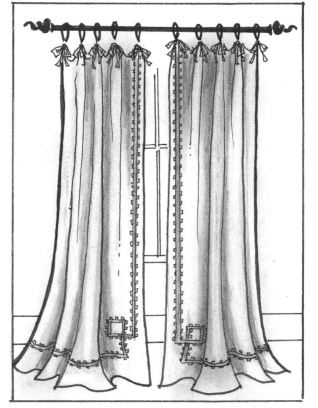

Add interest to a plain pair of curtains by adding a picot ribbon

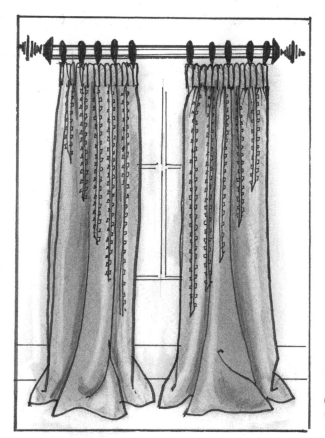

Use picot ribbons in different colours – looks great

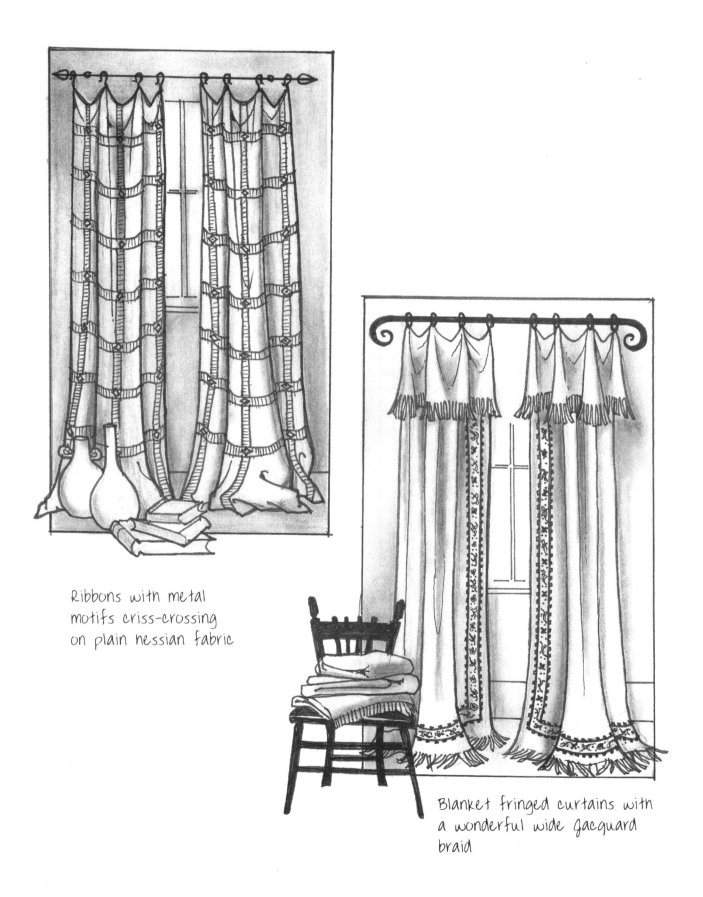

Ribbons with metal
motifs criss-crossing
on plain nessian fabric

Blanket fringed curtains with
a wonderful wide Jacquard
braid

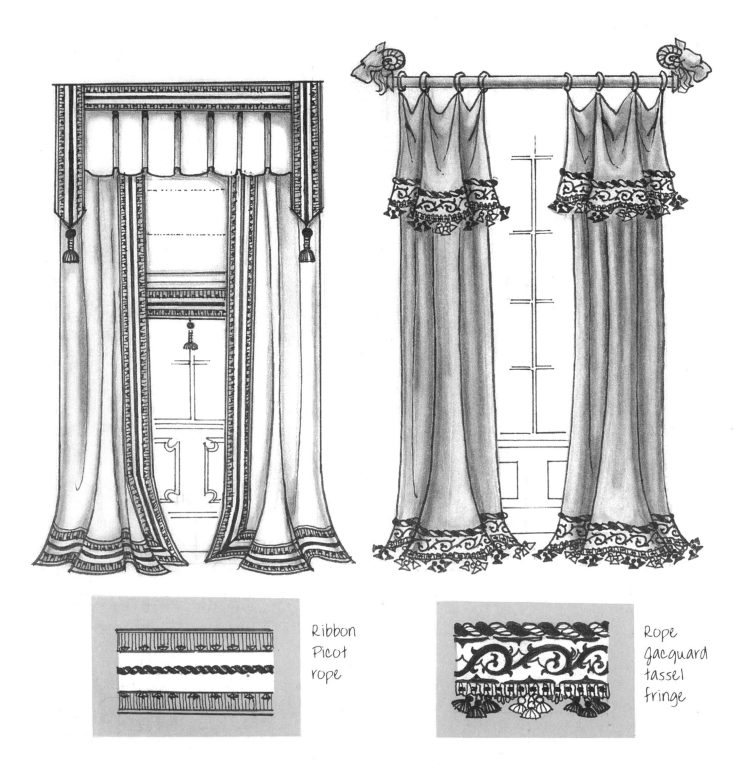

Ribbon
Picot
rope

Rope
Jacquard
tassel
fringe

Use a wide braid or ribbon as a base – add various other trimmings on top – this way
you can achieve a totally individual look –

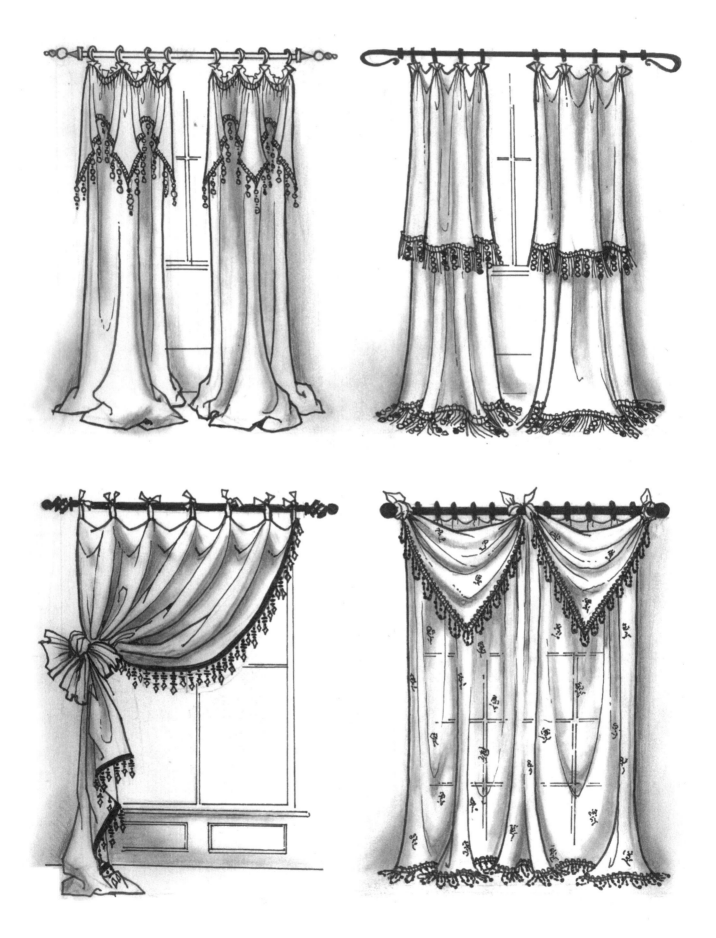

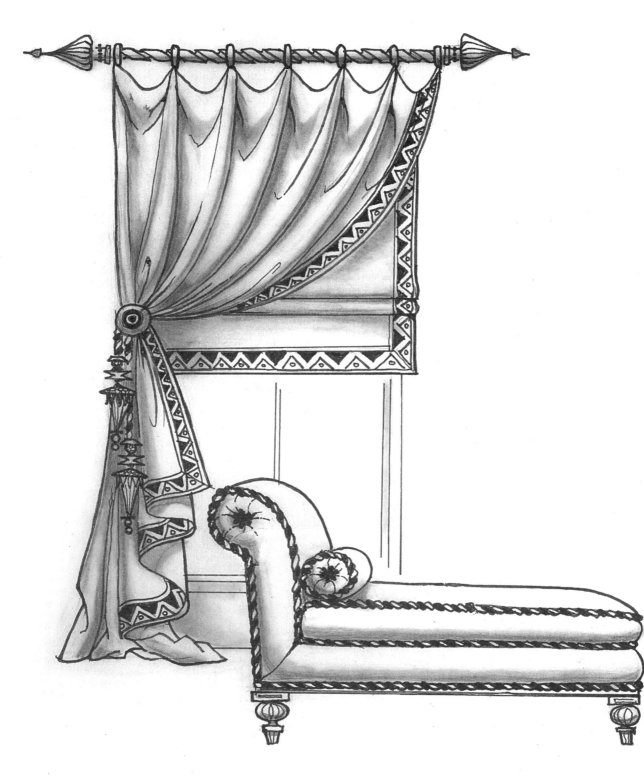

Just by adding that exotic wide braid the whole room is transformed

Take a window..

..add a curtain

or........

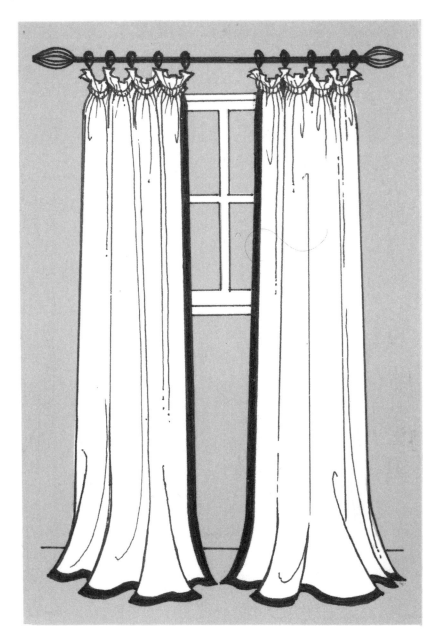

1. Stretch voile over the window

2. Hinged wooden frame with fabric to act as a shutter

3. Sandblast the glass in any patterns

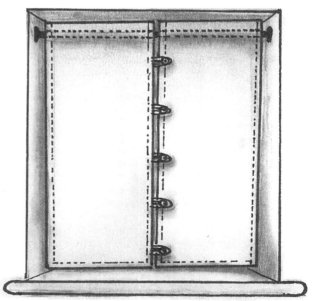

4. Two panels of fabric neatly buttoned up!

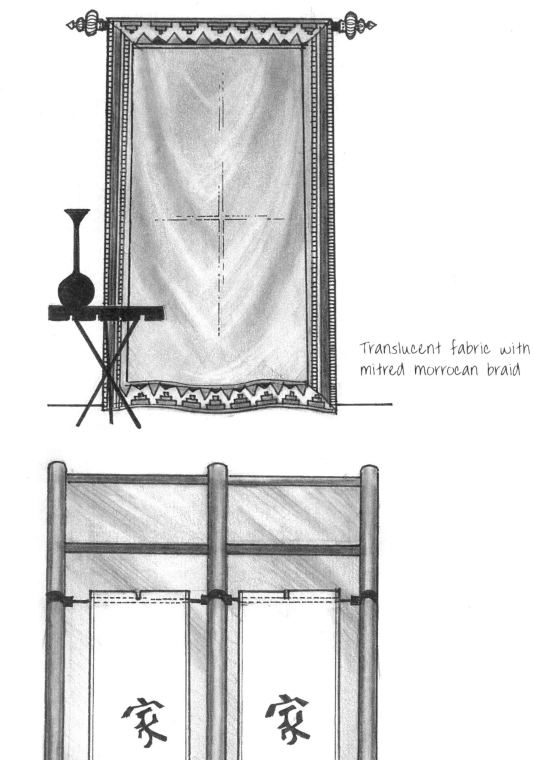

Translucent fabric with
mitred morrocan braid

Opaque cotton
panels

1.

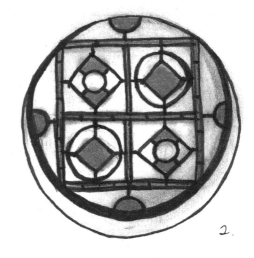

2.

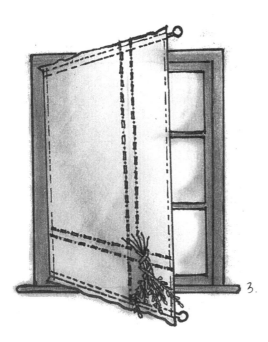

3.

1. Coloured panes of glass - and have fun by painting various objects on the other panes

2. Stain glass windows can be made in a multitude of patterns and colours

3. Linen slotted on to Portière rods and decorated with bugle beads

4. Two different patterned voile half - curtains slotted on to an iron pole in a recess window

5. Beaded curtain - thread on different coloured beads to make your own pattern

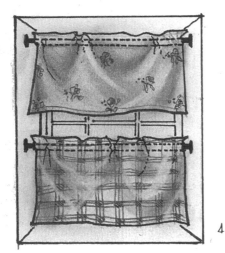

4.

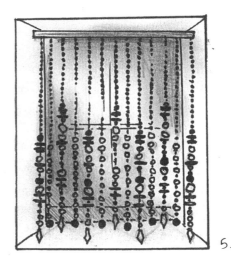

5.

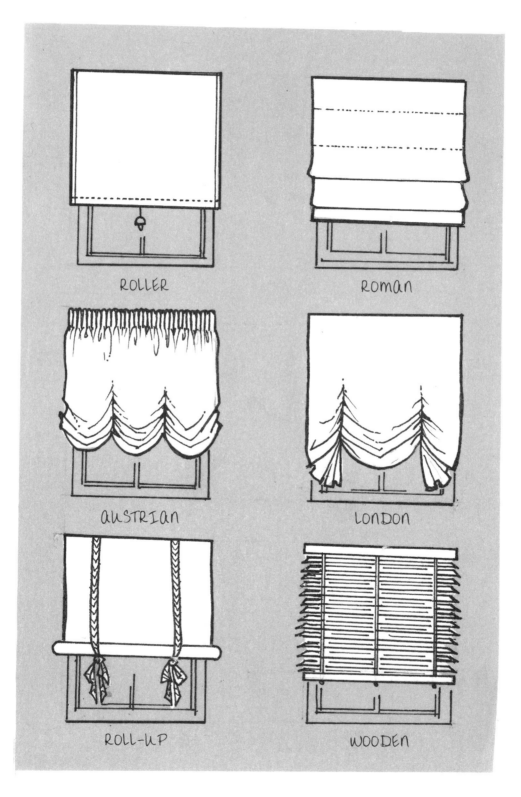

ROLLER

Roman

austrian

London

ROLL-UP

WOODEN

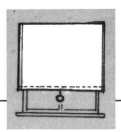

1.
2.
3.
4.
5.
6.

Pelmet

Lambrequins   –   with roller blinds

7.
8.
9.

Pull cords

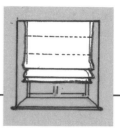

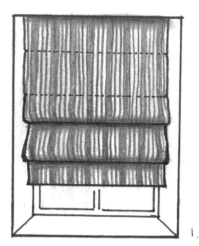

1.

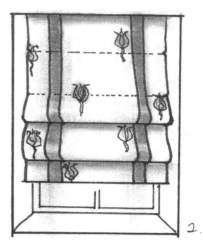

2.

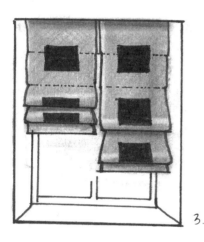

3.

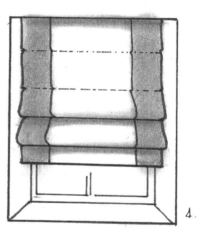

4.

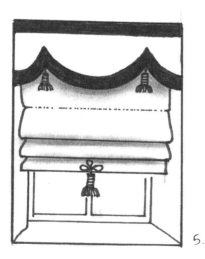

5.

6.

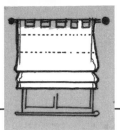

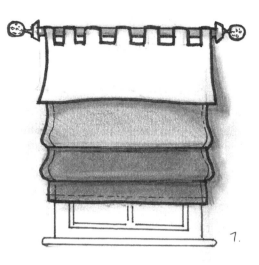

7.

8.

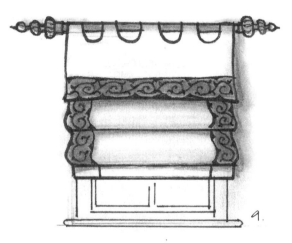

9.

10.

11.

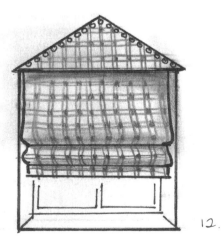

12.

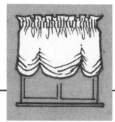

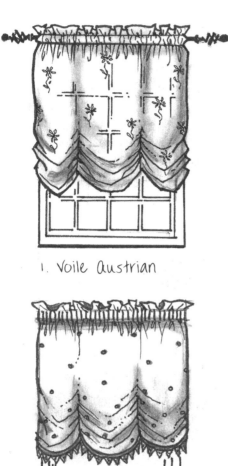

1. Voile Austrian

2. Crystal beaded edge

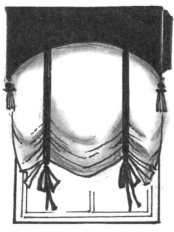

3. Laced edge

4. London blind

5. London blind
with pelmet

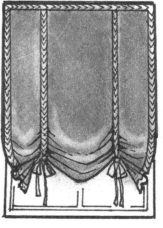

6. Wide chevron
jute braid

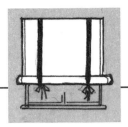

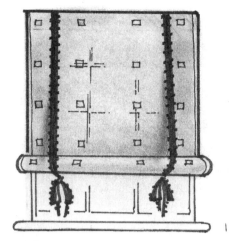

1.

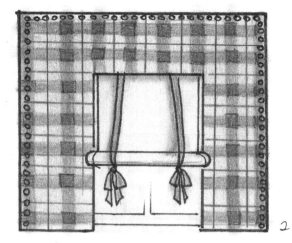

2.

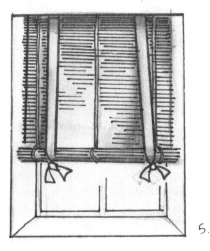

3.

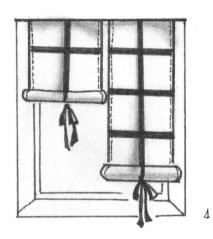

4.

5.

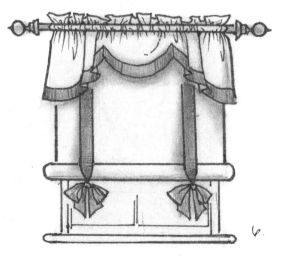

6.

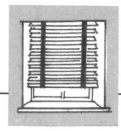

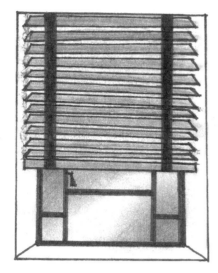

Woodslat blinds
with webbing

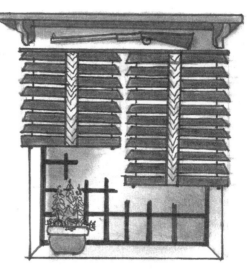

Leather blinds with
nessian webbing

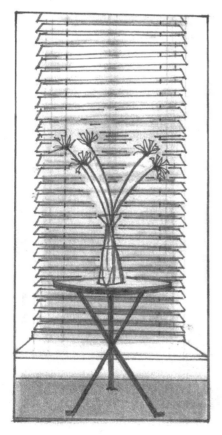

Venetian blinds
(wood or metal)

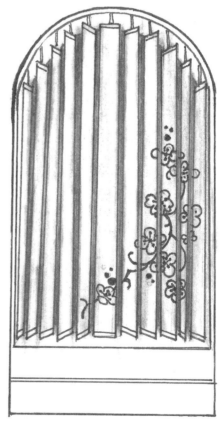

Vertical blinds
(cut to most shapes)

1.

2.

3.

4.

5.

6.

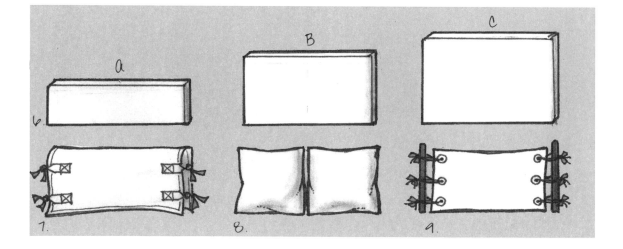

1. Simple throw over bed cover

2. Outline stitched quilt

3. Diamond stitched quilt with occasional knotted cotton ties

4. Throw over bed cover with knotted cotton ties, edged with a wide band of contrast fabric

5. Half American quilt with inverted pleated cotton valance

6. Delicate half lace bed cover with inverted pleated valance with ties

7. Plain fitted half bed cover with no shaping and with a straight valance

8. Pretty gingham bed coverlet with two rows of frills on the hem

Ruched and piped headboard with an outline quilt

Simple shaped and piped headboard with diamond stitched half quilt

Pretty cushioned back headboard – the curtain behind adds height to the room

This minimal cube shape can be achieved by using alternative coloured fabrics – preferably linen

Tall contemporary headboard covered in linen - blankets are satin edged
and blanket stitched

a contemporary suede or leather headboard edged with antiqued metal
studs - base to match

minimal style headboard with screen behind to add height. Tucked in
Harlequin bed cover

Deep buttoned velvet headboard with bed covers and cushions in rich prints and stripes. Use plenty of trimmings to achieve this exotic look

WOODEN BEDS

unusual shaped wooden bed with wide
painted lines to emphasise the shape –
American patchwork quilt

Simple planks of untreated wood for the bed and crisp cotton with lace for bed linen

Louis XV carved bed in natural wood finish or hand painted

An elegant interpretation of an antique
from the Third Empire, intricatley carved
wood and hand caned

Classic hand carved bed based on a 19th century antique French design

a truly decadent bed! Based on a Louis XVI design — hand carved
with a trellis and floral swag motif

solid wooden 'Lit Bateau' day-bed with an extra pull out bed below

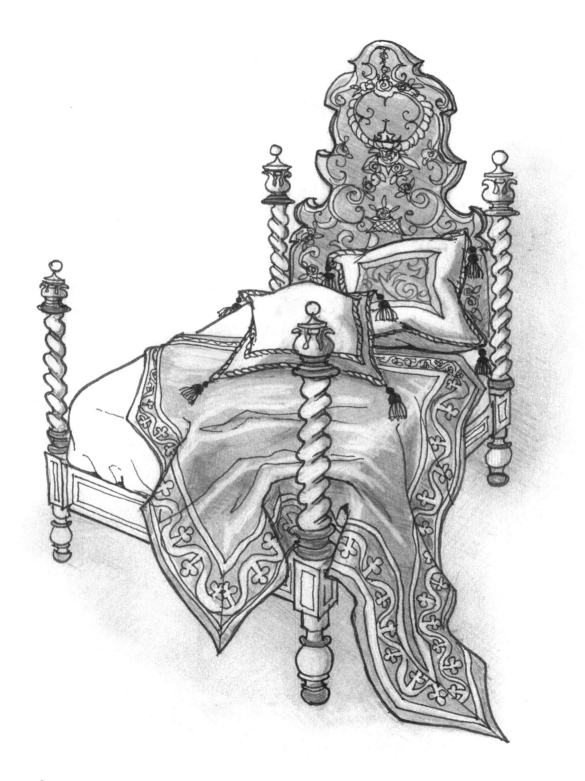

magnificent heavily carved moroccan style bed with a wide gold tapestry braid on the bed throw

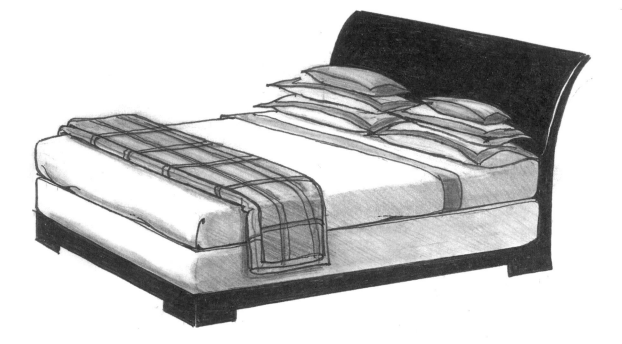

An elegant contemporary black polished wooden bed

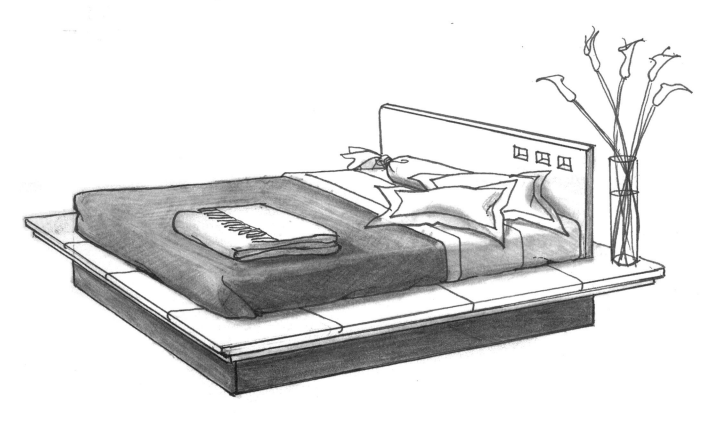

Simple cut-out headboard, bed with wooden shelf surround

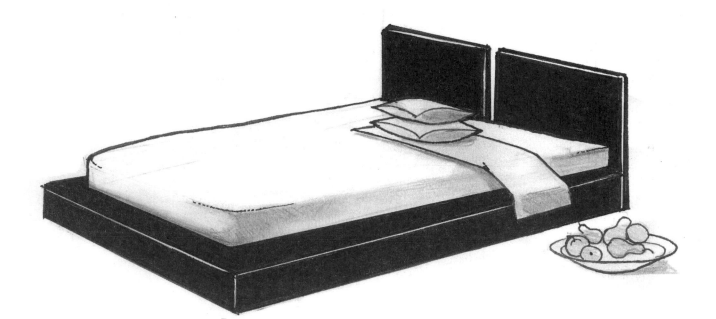

Double wooden headboard with base to match

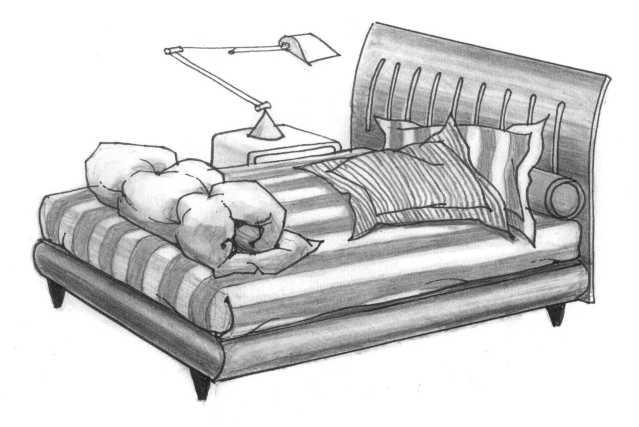

Slatted wood veneer headboard with wooden base

VARIATIONS ON IRON BEDS

Victorian style bed in iron
with brass top rail and knobs.
Crisp starched bed linen with
a soft rug - great in the
country farmhouse

This Gothic style bed
looks best in brushed
steel - the simple lines
lend itself to a modern
loft setting.

Iron bedstead with painted metal flowers - back curtain
can be plain or printed to match bedlinen

Brass bedstead with garlands of flowers and bows
Use plenty of lace on the bedlinen

Curvaceous bed with brass bed knobs - everyone's favourite

Bedstead with swirling ivy leaves in black iron looks really fabulous

Iron canopy bed - keep it simple or add
a twist of voile over the top rails to
bring an air of romance into the room

Iron corona with simple voile curtains attached with knotted ties

Basic corona with pencil heading – use mixture of stripes, checks and small flower prints

CORONAS

Double pinch pleated heading with square buttons and bullion fringing – use the same print as back curtain for outline quilt with roped hem

Gilded wooden corona with silk drapes edged with crystal beaded fringe

Gold leaf Empire corona with voile curtains and big soft bow. Ebony double-ended
wooden bed with starched white linen and cotton lace edging

Simple wooden corona with various trimmings and a mock animal skin as the cover

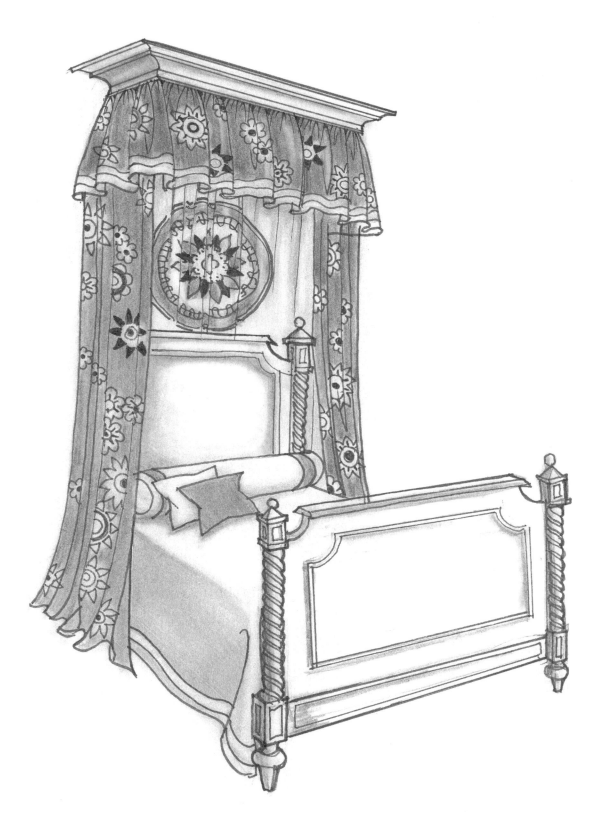

Traditional wooden pelmet with valance and side curtains - plain simple wooden bed

a large check fabric looks dynamic for this half-tester - add edging and tassels to emphasise the medieval shape

wooden Gothic pelmet with inverted pleats and heavy bullion fringing - add the
fringing also to the bed cover

Carved and gilded pelmet with tapestry valance and huge tassel tiebacks – carved headboard

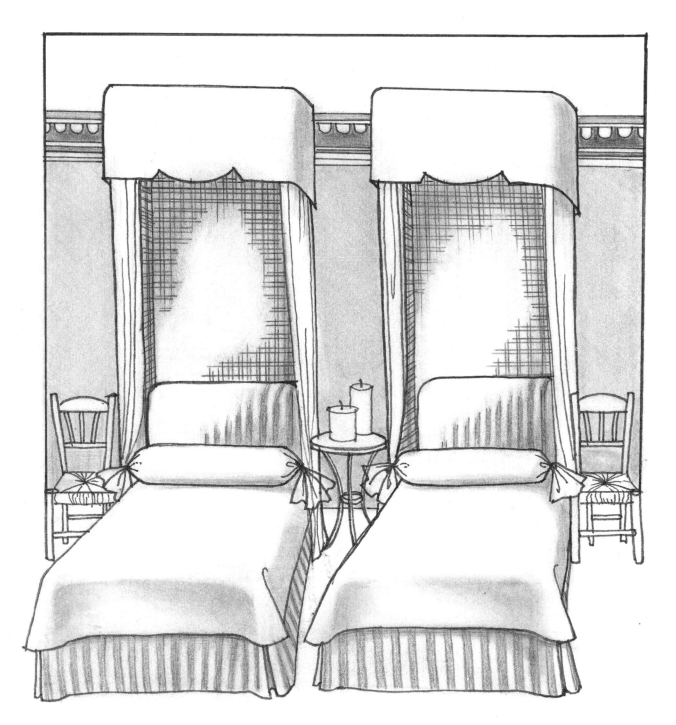

Two simple shaped tall half-testers – keep everything very plain and neat...

moroccan style half-tester with embroidery, fringing and topped with feathers

Oak four poster bed with fringed damask canopy - rope twists around
the wooden posts finally ending with large tassels

Wooden pelmet with skirt cut around the shape of the fabric design – heavily carved headboard – Egyptian cotton bedlinen

Carved and gilded pelmet - silk valance edged with delicate beaded
fringing - headboard and bed valance in silk striped fabric

Two toned knotted rope on the soft falling valance which is edged
with fabulous acorn fringing – use rope on all edges and tie
curtains back with acorn tassel tie-backs

Use an abundance of frilled paper taffeta fabric for
this flamboyant design - edge with delicate shades
of picot ribbons for a really soft feminine look

Heavy oak 'Tudor' style four poster with carved
wooden pelmet and fringed tassel valance

a traditional four poster with a modern twist - crisp cotton curtains
hang from the wooden curtain rings - white embossed bedcover

Carved wooden four poster - the curtains are twisted around the turned posts to give a more contemporay look

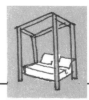

Simple black carved wooden bed – bed linen very plain – only colour comes from vibrant chevron throw at the end of the bed

Brushed steel four poster – two black suede headboards and
cushions – cream wool blanket and bolsters

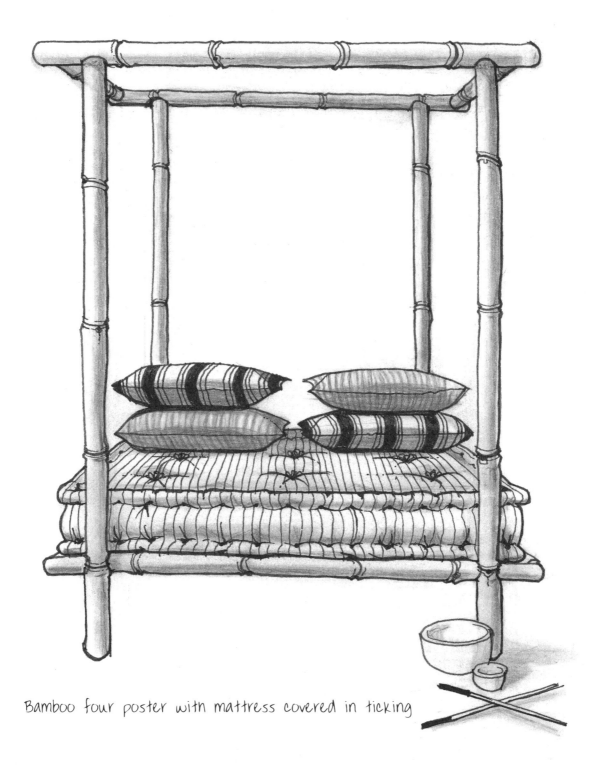

Bamboo four poster with mattress covered in ticking

wooden or steel bed - minimal design - piles of cushions in varying shades of grey

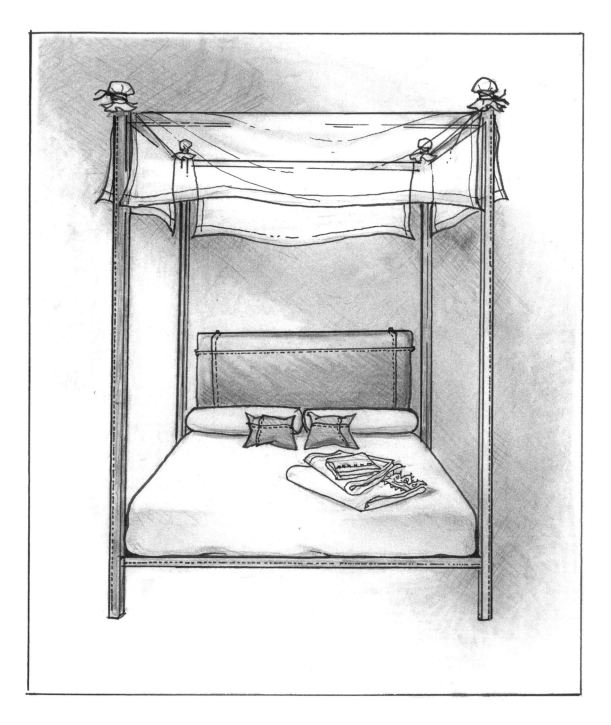

Suede covered four poster with suede headboard and cushions – knotted voile canopy

Iron four poster - double curtains on tab headings with square buttons - the check fabric inside matches the bed valance - half bed quilt with knots in cotton

Iron bed with shaped canopy top – colourful American throw

Dome shaped iron bed with double curtains in check and spot tied on with fabric ties

Steel four poster with brass knobs —
pastel crumpled silk fabric twists
around the pole and the 'housewife'
pillowcases are edged with faggotting

mock bamboo carved Colonial four poster – wide striped woollen blanket and fringed silk bed throw

wide colourful striped fabric suspended by wires from the ceiling –
choose a colour from the stripe to use for headboard and accessories

Simple iron four poster with striped canopy — use
the same fabric for headboards and bedcover

'Pretend' roll-up blinds used for this canopy bed – suspend them with ribbons from sky hooks

Pretty canopy with deep swags
caught up with gilt holdbacks -
use a soft flowing fabric and a
contrast inside the curtains

wooden frame suspended by
ropes — drape with voile
mosquito netting — two tall
padded headboards ... spectacular!

mosquito net canopy suspended
from ceiling – rolled-up bedcover
and 'mattress' cushions on a
printed Arabian silk throw

Child's cot - can be adapted later to a 'Lit Bateau' - has a delicate coronet with voile drapes held back with roses and bows

Child's wooden rocker in the shape of a teddy bear – hang checked voile from a hook for a pretty effect

Storage cupboards incorporating a bed for a little girl

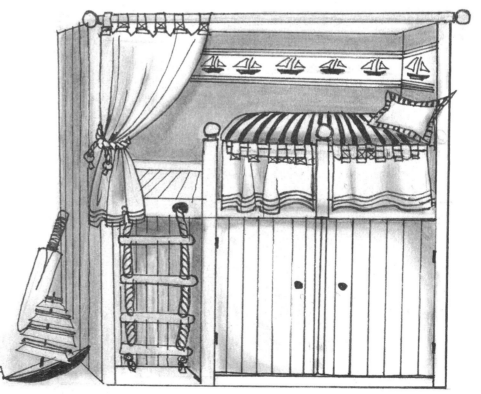

more storage with a bunk bed for a boy

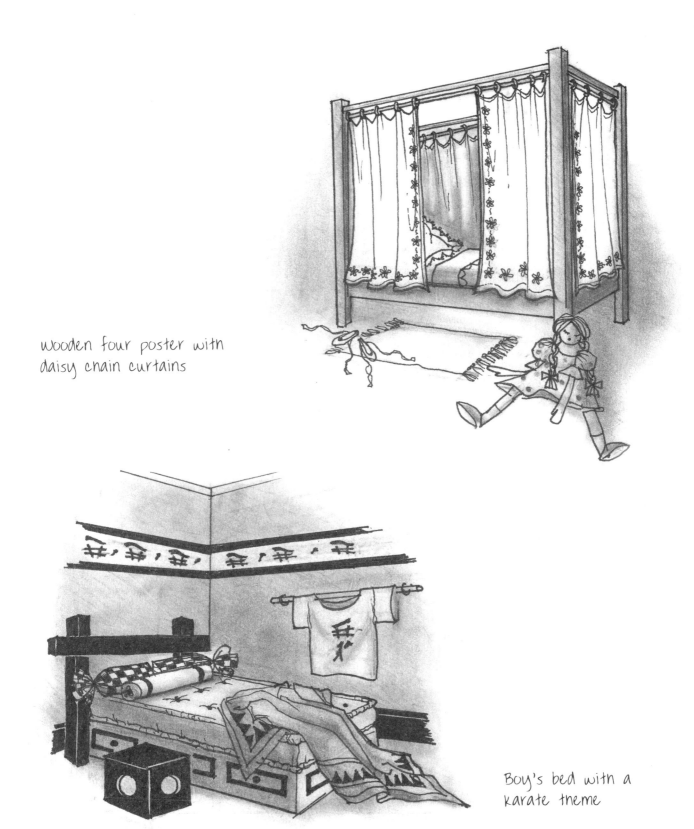

wooden four poster with
daisy chain curtains

Boy's bed with a
karate theme

Cosy alcove bed for teenage girl

Work station and storage
with bunk bed

Four poster bed with maypole ribbons and voile curtains for a teenage girl

Teenage boys bed with T.V. and 'sounds'

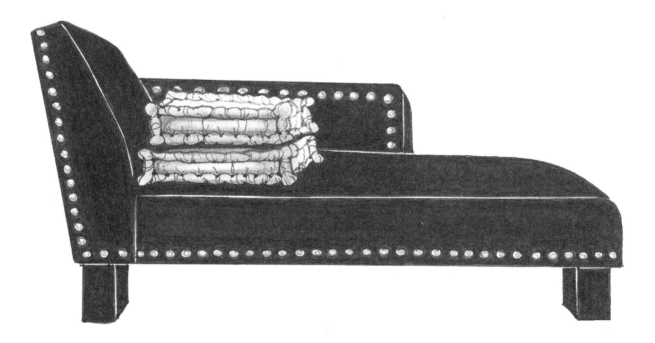

Suede day-bed with antique brass studding

Brown leather modern chaise longue

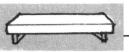

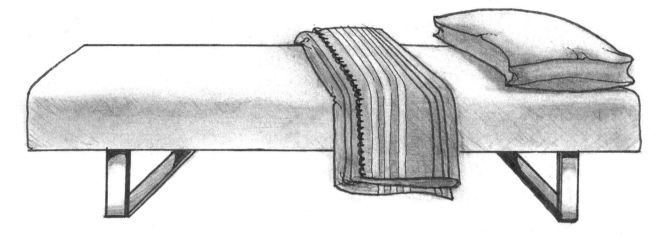

Basic modern day-bed – metal legs

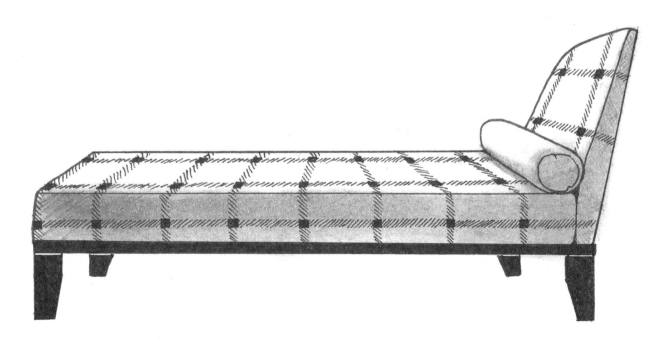

Day-bed in check fabric – with wooden legs

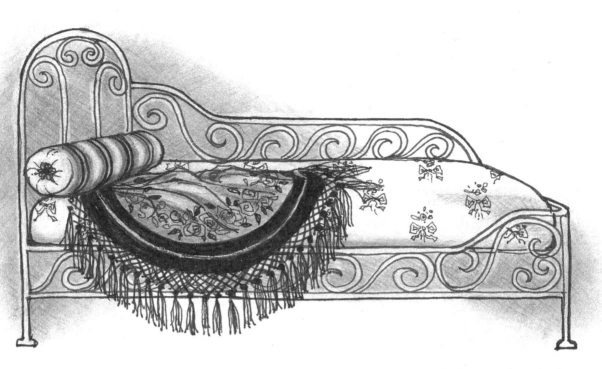

Painted iron day-bed

moroccan comfortable lounging bed

Hammock made from heavy woven Aztec fabric

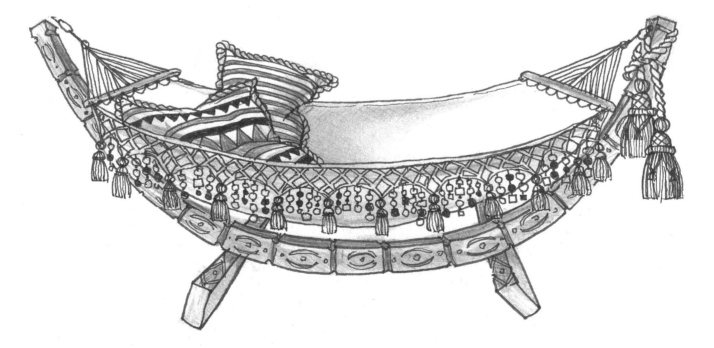

Beaded hammock hanging from a carved wooden base

Bamboo four poster set amongst the trees

mosquito tent hanging from a palm - that's the life...

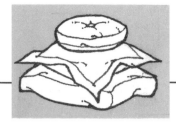

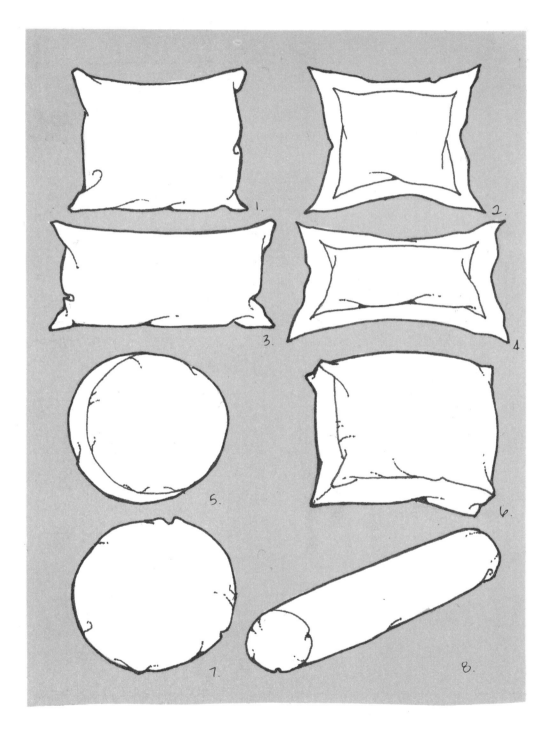

1.

2.

3.

4.

5.

6.

7.

8.

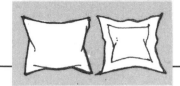

1.

2.

3.

4.

5.

6.

7.

8.

9.

10.

11.

12.

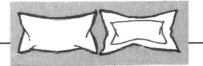

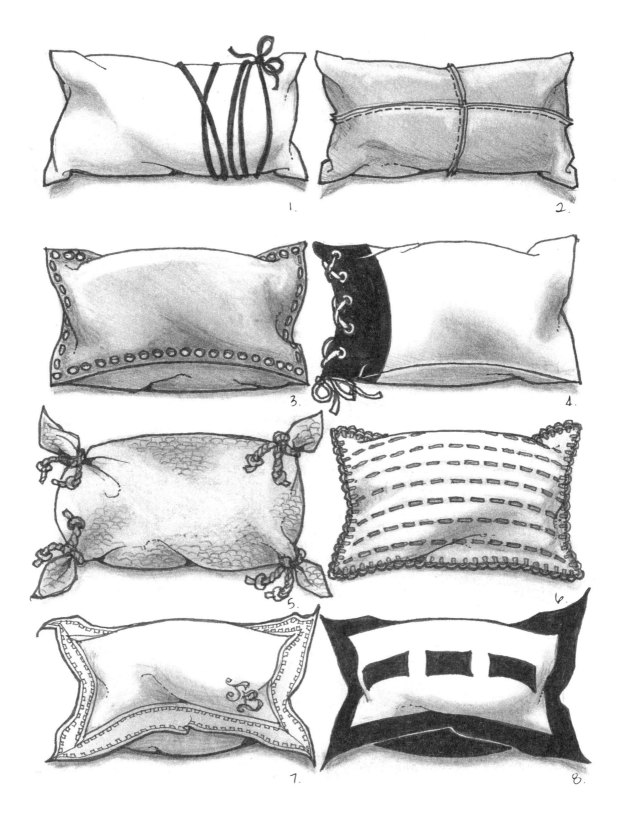

1.

2.

3.

4.

5.

6.

7.

8.

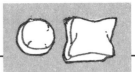

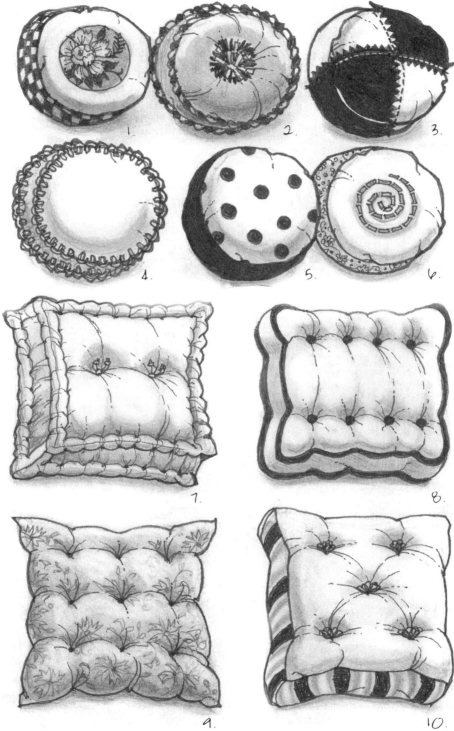

1.

2.

3.

4.

5.

6.

7.

8.

9.

10.

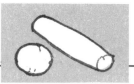

1.

2.

3.

4.

5.

6.

7.

8.

9.

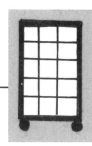

1. Huge bamboo roll-up blind with door opening

2. Split voile curtain with embossed printed picture

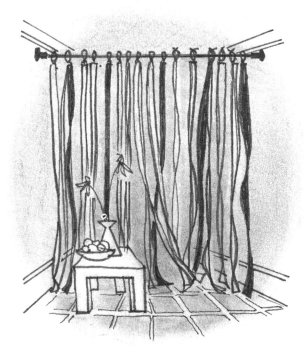

3. metal pole from wall to wall with various tied coloured ribbons

4. Room divider in glass with leaf impressions

5. Two dividers on wheels - wood with rice paper windows

1.

2.

3.

4.

5.

6.

7.

8.

9.

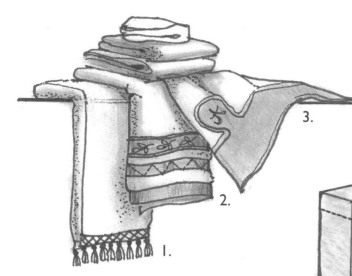

TOWELS

1. Tassel fringing
2. Various embroidered braids
3. Contrast satin edge with initials

SEATING

1. Leather pouffe with saddle-stitching
2. Plump suede knotted bean bag
3. Suede pouffe with animal fur fabric

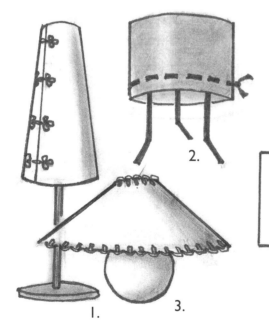

LIGHTING

1. Tall lampshade with frogging sides
2. Lampshade with leather thronging
3. Blanket stitched coolie lampshade
4. Cube lamp base and shade

5. Suede saddle-stitched lampshade
6. Lampshade trimmed with feathers
7. Standard lamp on metal tripod legs

SUPPLIERS UK

FABRICS

Below are names and telephone numbers of manufacturers of some of the best fabrics on the market. Telephone them for trade details and for stockists.

Anna French Tel: 020 7737 9608
Andrew Martin Tel: 020 7584 4290 (also modern furniture)
GP and J Baker Tel: 01494 467467
Bennison Tel: 020 7730 8076
Bernard Thorpe Tel: 020 7352 5745 (fabrics in your own colours)
Brian Yates Tel: 020 7352 0123
Brunschwig and Fils Tel: 020 7351 5797
Cath Kidston Tel: 020 7221 4000 (also childrens)
Chase Erwin Tel: 020 7352 7271
Colefax and Fowler Tel: 020 7351 0666
Conran Shop Tel: 020 7589 7401 (retail only)
Designers Guild Tel: 020 7351 5775
Donghia Tel: 020 7823 3456
Harvey and Nichols (retail) Tel: 020 7235 5000
Ian Mankin Tel: 020 7722 0997 (retail only-inexpensive Indian cotton)
Ian Sanderson Tel: 020 7351 2451
Jane Churchill Tel: 020 7361 0666
Jason D'Souza (Haywoods) Tel: 020 7351 4440
John Lewis Partnership Tel: 020 7828 1000 (retail only)
Laura Ashley Tel: 0870 562 2116
LeeJofa Tel: 020 7351 7760
Malibar Tel: 020 7501 4200
Mulberry Home (retail) Tel: 020 7235 5000
Nobilis Fontan Tel: 020 7351 7678
Osborne and Little Tel: 020 7352 1456
Percheron Tel: 020 7349 1590
J Robert Scott Tel: 020 7376 4705 (also contemporary furniture)
Robert Allen Tel: 01494 474741
Sanderson Tel: 01895 830000
Silk Gallery Tel: 020 7351 1790
Titley and Marr Tel: 020 7351 2913
Timney Fowler Tel: 020 7352 2263
Turnell and Gigon Tel: 020 7351 5142
Zimmer and Rohde Tel: 020 7351 7115
Zoffany Tel: 020 7349 0043

CURTAIN POLES - TRACKING - ACCESSORIES

Telephone for trade details and retail stockists

Bradley Collection (contemporary) Tel: 01449 722724
Byron and Byron Limited Tel: 020 8510 4800
Cope and Timmins Tel: 0845 458 8860
Edward Harpley Tel: 01449 737999 (also bespoke)
Eton and Oaks Tel: 01543 419468
Edward Harpley Tel: 01449 737999 (also bespoke)
Fabricant Limited Tel: 020 7263 7999
F.R. Street Tel: 01268 766677
Hallis Hudson Tel: 01772 909500
Hunter Hyland Tel: 01372 378511
Jim Lawrence (ironworks) Tel: 01206 263459
John Lewis Partnership (Retail only) - telephone for nearest store Tel: 020 7828 1000
MacCulloch and Wallis (accessories) Tel: 020 7629 0311
McKinney and Co. Tel: 020 7627 5077
Price and Co Tel: 01273 421999
Resina Designs Tel: 01934 863535
Robert Allen Tel: 01494 474741
Silent Gliss (contemporary tracking and blinds) Tel: 01843 863571
Swish Tel: 01827 64242
Tillys (contemporary poles) Tel: 023 9223 1143
Walcot House Limited Tel: 01993 832940 (contemporary poles and clips)

BLINDS AND SHUTTERS

Alison White (contemporary) Tel: 020 7609 6127
Blind Fashion Tel: 01628 529676
Hunter Douglas (also metal) Tel: 01698 887777
Plantation Shutters Tel: 020 8871 9333
Silent Gliss Tel: 01843 863 571
Swish Tel: 01827 64242
Tidmarsh and Sons (wooden) Tel: 020 7226 2261
The Shutter Shop (wooden) Tel: 020 7351 4204

NOTE: Most department stores sell blinds.

TRIMMINGS

(passementerie)
British Trimmings Tel: 0161 480 6122 (for stockists)
Colefax and Fowler Tel: 020 7351 0666
Henry Newbury Tel: 020 7636 5970
Jason D'Souza (Haywoods) Tel: 020 7351 4440
John Lewis (department store) Tel: 020 7828 1000 for nearest store
Osborne and Little Tel: 020 7352 1456
Turnell and Gignon (also bespoke) Tel: 020 7351 5142
Wendy Cushing Trimmings (also bespoke) Tel: 020 7351 5796
Wemyss (Houlès) Tel: 020 7255 3305
V.V. Rouleaux Tel: 020 7730 3125

BED MANUFACTURERS

Dragons of Walton Street (children's beds) Tel: 020 7589 3795
Iron Bed Company Tel: 01243 578888
James Adam (wooden) Tel: 01394 384471
Kynes Feather Bed Company Tel: 0121 680 7366
Savoir Beds (handmade) Tel: 020 8838 4838
Seventh Heaven (antique) Tel: 01691 777622
Simon Horn (wooden and antique) Tel: 020 7731 1279
The French House (antique) Tel: 01787 477346

NOTE: All major stores have bed departments: look out for these leading bed manufacturers:

REYLON
STAPLES
VI-SPRING
HYPNOS

BED LINEN -

pillows and accessories

Conran Tel: 020 7589 7401
Damask Tel: 020 7736 4638
Frette Tel: 020 7491 2750
Habitat Tel: 020 7351 1211
John Bell Croydon Tel: 020 7935 5555 (medical support beds)
Lunn Antiques Tel: 020 7736 4638
White House Tel: 020 7629 8269

NOTE: All major department stores stock bed linen.

NOTE: When in London visit **Chelsea Harbour Design Centre**, Lots Road, London SW10. Tel: 020 7225 9100 There are many fabrics and furniture companies all under one roof.

FABRICS

Anna French Tel: 617 574 9030
Brunschwig and Fils
Tel: 212 838 7878
Christopher Norman
Tel: 212 644 4100
Colefax and Fowler
Tel: 212 753 4488
Cowan and Tout
Tel: 212 753 4488
Designers Guild Tel: 212 751 3333
Donghia Tel: 1 800 DONGHIA
Fonthill Tel: 212 755 6700
Hinson and Co Tel: 212 475 4100
J Robert Scott Tel: 212 755 4910
**Jane Churchill and Manual
Canovas** - see Colefax and Fowler
Lee Jofa Tel: 212 688 0444
Osborne and Little (Nina Campbell)
Tel: 212 751 3333
Ralph Lauren (US stockist call
1 800 578 7656
Robert Allen Tel: 212 421 1200
Schumacher and Co
Tel: 212 415 3900
Travers and Co Tel: 212 888 7900
Zimmer and Rohde
Tel: 212 627 8880

SPECIALIST STORES for
fabrics and accessories -
telephone for nearest store

Calico Corners Tel: 610 444 9700
Home Depot Expo
Tel: 770 433 8211
Jo-Ann Tel: 330 463 6790

CURTAIN POLES
(Drapery Hardware)

ABC Carpet and Home
Tel: 212 473 3000
Calico Corners Tel: 610 444 9700
(call for stockists)
Carleton Limited (trade)
Tel: 212 355 4525
Gracious Home (and accessories)
Tel: 212 231 7800
Houlès Tel: 212 935 3900
Home Depot Expo
Tel: 770 433 8211
Joseph Biunno (finials unlimited)
Tel: 212 629 5630
Jo-Ann Tel: 330 4636 790
Kirch (trade and retail)
Tel: 1-800 817 6344
Robert Allen Tel: 1-800 3020

TRIMMINGS
(Passementerie)

M & J Décor (trade)
Tel: 212 704 8000
Passementerie Inc
Tel: 212 355 7600
Fonthill Tel: 212 755 6700
Robert Allen Tel: 1 800 333 3777
Donghia Tel: 1-800 DONGHIA
Houlès Tel: 212 935 3900
Christopher Norman
Tel: 212 644 4100
Conso Products Co
Tel: 864 427 9004

BED STORES/
MANUFACTURERS

ABC Carpet and Home (store)
Tel: 212 473 3000
Avery Boardman (beds and
Headboards) Tel: 1 800 501 4850
Bed, Bath & Beyond
Tel: 212 255 3550
Charles P Rogers (brass and iron)
Tel: 212 675 4400
Kid's Supply Co Tel: 212 426 1200
Kleinsleep Bedding (discount)
Tel: 212 755 8210
Macy's (Store) Tel: 212 695 4400
Simon Horn Limited (wooden)
Tel: 205 876 6222

NOTE: Look for these good makes
of beds in stores.

STEARNS AND FOSTER
SEALY (POSTUREPEDIC)
SIMMONS

Or for info Tel: 1-800 MATTRESS

BED LINEN
sheets-pillowcases-shams

ABC Carpet and Home
Tel: 212 473 3000
Anichini Tel: 1-800 553 5309
Bloomingdales (store)
Tel: 212 705 2000
Freete (luxury)
Tel: 212 473 3000 (ext 723)
Macy's (store) Tel: 212 695 4400
Schweitzer Linens
Tel: 212 249 8361
Takashimaya (luxury)
Tel: 212 350 0100

BLINDS

Window Modes (bamboo)
Tel: 212 752 1140
The Workroom Tel: 212 688 4644

NOTE: Most stores sell blinds and
shutters.

NOTE:
TRADE CENTERS

D & D Building
979 Third Avenue
New York
NY 10022
Tel: 212 759 2964

Design Center
200 Lexington Avenue
New York
NY 10016
Tel: 212 679 9500

ATLANTA - Design Center
Tel: 404 231 1720

SAN FRANCISCO - Design Center
Tel: 415 864 1500

DALLAS - Design Center
Tel: 214 747 2411

SEATTLE - Design Center
Tel: 800 497 7997

PACIFIC - Design Center
Tel: 310 657 0800